Words of Love

Spoken by Our Lord to
Three Twentieth-Century Victim Souls:

Sister Josefa Menendez,
Sister Mary of the Trinity,
and Sister Consolata Betrone

Compiled by
Father Bartholomew Gottemoller, o.c.s.o.

> *"That being rooted and founded in charity, you may be able to comprehend, with all the saints, what is the breadth, and length, and height and depth: to know also the charity of Christ, which surpasseth all knowledge, that you may be filled unto all the fulness of God."*
> —Ephesians 3:17-19

TAN BOOKS AND PUBLISHERS, INC.
Rockford, Illinois 61105

Nihil Obstat: Rev. John Hedderman, J.C.L.
                     Censor Deputatus

Imprimatur: ✟ Joseph Lennox Federal
                     Bishop of Salt Lake City
                     December 2, 1971

First edition published by Abbey of the Holy Trinity, Huntsville, Utah. Revised, typeset, and republished by TAN Books and Publishers, Inc.

Library of Congress Catalog Card No.: 84-51596

ISBN: 0-89555-244-2

Printed and bound in the United States of America.

TAN BOOKS AND PUBLISHERS, INC.
P.O. Box 424
Rockford, Illinois 61105

1985

"It is the sun that gives the earth its beauty and animates it. It is My grace that gives souls their beauty and that animates them. My Omnipotence is limited only by your liberty. It is with coal that I make diamonds. What would I not do with a soul, however black she might be, who would give herself to Me."

—*Words of Our Lord*
to Sister Mary of the Trinity

CONTENTS

CONTENTS

PREFACE

This book consists of words of Christ given in private revelations to three victim souls; the excerpts included herein are taken from three different books. In one important respect, all three books are very much alike: Each one deals with the life and intimate relations of a holy nun with Christ, and each of these nuns was chosen by God as an instrument through whom He willed to convey a special message to the world. Because the message of Our Lord to these three nuns is strikingly similar, it has been thought useful to gather together selected quotations from all three sources, grouping them by topic.

It is true that private revelations must not be given that credence which is due to the word of God as contained in Holy Scripture; all private revelations must be judged according as they conform to human reason and to Divine Revelation as interpreted by the Church.

However, private revelations should be given that respect and credence which is fittingly due to any spiritual writing according to its intrinsic value. And the fact that such words may proceed from a special intervention on God's part should make us approach them with even more respect and openness. Indeed, private revelations seem to be God's way of putting the ancient Gospel truths into our modern form of expression. To realize this one has only to compare private revelations of the past with those of the present.

The three sources from which the excerpts in this book were taken are:

The Way of Divine Love, or *The Message of the Sacred Heart to the World,* which presents the life and message of Sister Josefa Menendez, published by TAN Books and Publishers, Inc.

The Spiritual Legacy of Sister Mary of the Holy Trinity, edited by Rev. Silvere Van Den Broek, O.F.M., published by TAN Books and Publishers, Inc.

Jesus Appeals to the World, by Lorenzo Sales, I.M.C., which presents the message of Sister Consolata Betrone, published by Alba House and available from TAN Books and Publishers, Inc.

The three nuns are designated in the text thus:
J.M. —Sister Josefa Menendez
M.T.—Sister Mary of the Holy Trinity
C.B. —Sister Consolata Betrone

The compiler and the publisher hope that these beautiful words of Our Lord will be an occasion of countless graces for many souls and that many readers will be inspired to go on to read the full books from which these marvelous excerpts were taken.

INTRODUCTION

Sister Josefa Menendez

Josefa was born in Madrid, Spain, on February 4, 1890, of good Catholic parents of moderate means. She was the eldest of four surviving children. When her father died, she became the sole support of the family through her skillful sewing. By nature she was both serious and vivacious.

When preparing for her First Communion at the age of eleven, she resolved to give herself entirely to God. It was then that she heard a voice for the first time saying to her, "Yes, little one, I want you to be all Mine." She was twenty-nine before she was able finally to achieve her desired goal of entering the Society of the Sacred Heart.

As the sisters of the Sacred Heart were opening a new novitiate at their convent of Les Feuillants, in Poitiers, France, she agreed to go there for her novitiate, thus making the sacrifice of her native land.

During her novitiate and short religious life she had great temptations against her vocation. The devil seemed determined to make her leave, and she was able to persevere and make her first vows only with the greatest difficulty. Her final vows were made on her death bed.

Even when Sister Josefa was a novice, God began to intervene in her life in an extraordinary way. Her religious life became one series of extraordinary communications with the supernatural world, although no one ever came to know of this except her superiors and her confessor. Her obedience, simplicity, and detachment were admirable and sure signs that she was being led by God. Her great temptation, up to the very end, was to withdraw from this extraordinary way of God's special choosing and to be allowed to go by an ordinary way that would leave her free for her work. She feared this way chosen for her by God, and only consented to it as an inescapable manifestation of the divine will.

Our Lord willed to use Josefa to manifest to souls, by the visible supernatural love and mercy He showed to her, that invisible love and care which He has for all souls. It is as

Sister Josefa Menendez
Coadjutrix Sister of the
Society of the Sacred Heart of Jesus
1890-1923

though Jesus were saying to us: "Do you see how I love and care for this chosen soul? Well, I am loving and caring for you just as much, but in a hidden and unseen way. Believe and trust in My love and mercy."

Our Lord also desired that Josefa give Him other souls. He led her in the ways of a victim soul, wherein she won graces for others. Our Lord told Josefa that her "littleness and sufferings" had saved many souls.

This was part of the message that God willed to give to the world through her, but He also willed to give through her a written message, one written down at His own dictation. The writing of this, together with the account of all her supernatural relations with God, was done out of obedience to her superiors. This was very painful to Josefa and something that cost her very much in the way of self-denial.

Josefa's death, at the age of thirty-three, on December 29, 1923, was as extraordinary and as hidden as her life had been. Only after her death did those with whom she lived learn of the extraordinary life which she had lived in their midst. Cardinal Pacelli (later Pope Pius XII), who was Cardinal Protector of the Society at the time, wrote a letter of commendation for the published account of her life.

Anyone who has received a favor through the intercession of Sister Josefa Menendez is asked to report it to the Sacred Heart Convent, Mount Anville, Dublin 14, Ireland.

Sister Mary of the Trinity

Sister Mary (Louisa Jaques) was born in 1901 of French-Swiss, Protestant parents in Pretoria, Transvaal, South Africa, where her father was a missionary. Shortly after her birth, the family returned to Switzerland. From early childhood she was a very affectionate girl and had a great love for her family.

At one point in her life she experienced a loss of faith in the existence of God. It was at that moment that she had a vision of a nun, which moved her to begin to cherish a secret desire to go and pray in a convent—that is, to go and become a religious. She began visiting churches, and in time, God in His providence brought her into the Catholic Church, especially through an intense desire to receive Christ in Holy Communion. Once a Catholic, she longed and prayed for the conversion of her family.

She did not immediately follow her desire to be a nun; actually, she had a fear of doing so. However, after experiencing a rather striking cure, she started in earnest to look for a convent to enter. There followed a nightmare of attempts: She was refused by many, accepted only for a while by others, but unable to attain her goal in any of them. Finally, while on a pilgrimage to the Holy Land, where she had heard there was a convent of Poor Clares, she stopped to pray in their chapel. This was in Jerusalem. God brought about Sister Mary's entrance there in June 1938 with an ease that clearly manifested His hand. She was to live only four more years.

Our Lord never appeared to Sister Mary of the Holy Trinity; she only heard His inner voice speaking to her. This had happened several times before she entered, but in the convent it became more frequent. Her confessor ordered her to write down what Our Lord said to her, and thus it is that we have a record of her experiences during the last two years of her life.

For her also Our Lord had a special mission. He asked her to make a vow to be a victim soul, saying that others would follow her in this. His words were: "I desire a great army of victim souls who will join Me in the apostolate of My Eucharistic life, who will bind themselves to Me by the vow of victim to choose the methods which I chose." (No. 363). "I ask four things of the souls who bind themselves more closely to Me by the vow of victim: 1) To listen to Me more than to speak to Me; 2) To strive to reproduce My actions, My way of acting, rather than My words; 3) To be before men as they are before God, in a state of poverty that begs, not in a state of spiritual wealth that gives alms of its superfluity . . . ; 4) To confine their efforts to spreading My Spirit, My gentleness, and My kindness which does not dwell on evil, but overcomes evil by good; . . . being exacting with no one but themselves. . . ." (No. 366).

Our Lord had foretold the early death of Sister Mary of the Trinity; she died on June 25, 1942, after a short illness. Anyone who has obtained a favor through the intercession of Sister Mary of the Trinity is asked to write to The Poor Clares, Corpus Christi Monastery, 2111 South Main St., Rockford, Illinois 61102.

Sister Mary of the Trinity
Poor Clare of Jerusalem
1901-1942

Sister Consolata Betrone

Sister Consolata (Pierina Betrone) was born April 6, 1903, at Saluzzo, Italy. Her parents moved to Turin a year later.

At the age of thirteen she heard for the first time, after Communion, an inner voice asking, "Do you wish to be entirely Mine?" She replied, "Yes, Jesus." By being "entirely Mine," she understood becoming a nun. This she strove hard to achieve, and finally she was received in the Capuchin convent of Turin. Ten years later she passed to their new convent at Moriondo.

Although she was favored by God with great spiritual gifts, these passed unobserved in her small community. She had many struggles with temptations and her own shortcomings, but with God's help she overcame them. Her way of spiritual life was very much like that of St. Therese the Little Flower, whose disciple she became. In fact, it was the reading of the *Story of a Soul* that actually urged her on to give herself to God in religion.

God led Sister Consolata into a new aspect of the practice of the "Little Way." She was moved to see herself as that "still weaker soul" for whom the Little Flower promised that God would work even greater marvels. That she was this soul Christ affirmed on November 27, 1935, saying, "Well, I have found that still weaker soul who has abandoned herself with complete faith to My infinite mercy: it is you, Consolata, and through you I will perform marvels which will far exceed your fondest desires."

Christ instructed her in the practice of what He called "the unceasing act of love," expressed in the words, "Jesus, Mary, I love you! Save souls!" Of this prayer, Our Lord said, "Tell Me, what more beautiful prayer do you want to offer Me? 'Jesus, Mary, I love you! Save souls!' Love and souls! What more beautiful prayer could you desire?" In addition to this prayer, He required two other things of her. She was to have a smiling "Yes" for everyone, seeing and dealing with Jesus in everyone; she was to have a grateful "Yes" for everything that happened to her or was required of her.

In time it became evident that God intended to use her to transmit a message to the world. On July 4, 1936, Jesus said to her, "Among the youngest members of Catholic action there are the Little Ones, and among the Little souls there are the Littlest Ones. You belong to these; and to them will

Sister Consolata Betrone
Capuchin
1903-1946

belong all those souls who will follow you in offering Me the unceasing act of love.''

The first soul to consecrate herself to this "Littlest Way" was Giovanna Compaire at the age of 85, thus showing that it is *spiritual* littleness that is meant. Her life was completely rejuvenated by her offering and she died a very holy death. She was the first, but not the last, to make this offering, for Our Lord promised that millions of both men and women would consecrate themselves to this "Littlest Way." The ejaculation, "Jesus, Mary, I love you! Save souls!" is now known and prayed throughout the world.

Sister Consolata died a holy death on July 18, 1946, at the age of 43. To report graces received through her intercession, write to her convent: Monastero Sacro Cuore, Clarisse Cappuccine, 10027 Testona Tor., Italia.

ABANDONMENT IN GENERAL

"As you are very small, you must let yourself be controlled and guided by My fatherly hand which is powerful and infinitely strong. . . . I will mold you as is best for My glory and for souls. . . . Do not fear, for I am looking after you with jealous care, such care as the tenderest of mothers takes of her little child." *(J.M., p.180).*

"One act of abandonment glorifies Me more than many sacrifices." *(J.M., p.210).*

"Do you think that anything happens without My permission? I dispose all things for the good of each and every soul." *(J.M., p.331).*

"Ah! Josefa, leave yourself, such as you are, to My care, and let the sight of your nothingness never lessen your trust, but only confirm you in humility." *(J.M., p.343).*

"Do not worry, Josefa, about what you can and what you cannot do. You know very well that you can do nothing. But I am He who can and will do all. Yes, I will do all, even what seems to you impossible. . . . I will supply for all that you lack or cannot do. I ask you only for your liberty. All I need is to possess your will, for this I cannot find a substitute." *(J.M., p.401, 1st ed.).*

[St. Madeleine-Sophie Barat]: "I come to tell you this from Him . . . Jesus Himself is arranging everything, and difficult as it may appear to creatures, He ordains each event in the way best for His plans." *(J.M., p.433).*

"I want you to be always abandoned and happy, because My Heart cares for you tenderly." *(J.M., p.133).*

[Josefa]: "There is but one thing to do: love and abandon

oneself. Jesus Himself will take charge of all the rest. . . ."
(J.M., p.27).

"Let yourself be led blindfold. My eyes are wide open to lead
you, and am I not your Father?" *(J.M., p.394).*

"He who gives his life to the Eternal Wisdom does not need
to be clever. Think only of Me, of pleasing Me: I will
transform you." *(M.T., no. 9).*

"Rely on Me with closed eyes, without anxiety, content . . .
yes, like a babe sleeping in its mother's arms. Are you not
like babes carried in the arms of God?" *(M.T., no. 265).*

"You are in God, in His Power, as leaves abandoned to a
breath of wind." *(M.T., no. 550).*

"I want what you do not want, but I can do what you cannot
do. It is not for you to choose, but to surrender." *(J.M., p.78).*

"Look, Consolata, people are accustomed to measure the
virtue of a soul by the graces which I grant her, but they
deceive themselves, for I am free to act as I please. For
example, does your virtue merit the great graces which I
have granted you? Poor Consolata, you have no virtue, you
have no merits, you have nothing! You would have your sins,
but they exist no more, for I have forgotten them for all
eternity. Why then so many, many graces for you in
particular? Because I am free to do good to whom I will. The
little ones are My weakness—that explains everything! . . .
And no one can accuse Me of injustice, for a sovereign is free
to bestow his royal favors on whom he will." *(C.B., p.26-27).*

"You must think only of loving Me! I will think of everything
else, even to the smallest details!" *(C.B., p.109).*

"Consolata, you know that I am thinking of everything, that
I am providing for everything down to the smallest detail.
Therefore, do not let one thought enter your mind, not one
outside interest. . . . Have no fear! I am taking care of you!"
(C.B., p.109).

"Remember this: Everything is a means in My Hands; I

make all work together to fulfill My will." *(M.T., no. 132)*.

"If you could but understand My joy when souls leave Me free and by their deeds say: 'Lord, Thou art the Master!' Do you realize how much this comforts Me? Do you think that I am not glorified by it?" *(J.M., p.210)*.

"A soul who truly surrenders herself to Me gives Me so much joy that in spite of her miseries and imperfections she becomes a very heaven of delight to Me and I take pleasure in abiding in her." *(J.M., p.86)*.

~2~

ABANDONMENT
"Let Me Act"

"Let Me act; you are not competent to do anything; it is not your province." *(M.T., no. 114).*

[Regarding Josefa:] "And when she told Him how worn out she was by the weeks of pain she had gone through: 'I have no need of your strength, but I do need your surrender,' He answered tenderly." *(J.M., p.154).*

"Consolata, I delight in you because I can do everything I wish, and it is I who am doing everything. You know with what care and affection a mother makes a little dress for her infant; she really puts her whole heart into it. But if the child were not to let her make the dress because he wanted to make it himself, that would sadden the mother." *(C.B., p.29).*

"You see, Consolata, sanctity means self-forgetfulness in everything, in thoughts, desires, words ... Allow Me to do it all! I will do everything; but you should, at every moment, give Me what I ask for with much love!" *(C.B., p.153).*

"Consolata, I have every claim upon you, but you have only one duty: to obey Me. I require a docile will which permits Me to act, which lends itself to everything, which trusts in Me and serves Me always in peace and joy, no matter what the situation is." *(C.B., p.154).*

"Let Me do everything! You will see that I will do everything, and do it well, and that My little victim will become fruitful in love and in souls!" *(C.B., p.154).*

"I delight to work in a soul. You see, I love to do everything Myself; and from this soul I ask only that she love Me." *(C.B., p.154).*

4

"My little daughter, if you endeavor to speak to Me, your voice might drown Mine . . . It is better to keep a respectful silence that allows you to listen to Me." *(M.T., no. 305).*

"Think no longer about yourself, about your perfection, on how to attain to sanctity, or about your defects, your present and future troubles. No. I will see to your sanctification, to your sanctity. You must henceforth think only of Me and of souls; of Me to love Me, and of souls to save them!" *(C.B., p.155).*

"The most important work is not that which you do, it is that which you allow Me to do among you." *(M.T., no. 31).*

"Your value does not lie in your personal capabilities, however brilliant they may be, but in your capacity to receive your Creator and allow Him to live and shine through you." *(M.T., no. 90).*

"Oh, if you would leave Me to act; I would splendidly transform each one of your lives. But you oppose Me by your desires, your tastes, your resistance. My omnipotent Love is limited by the limit of your generosity." *(M.T., no. 99).*

"It is because you are nothing that I can take possession of you, substitute Myself for you. Oh, how I thirst for souls— how I long for them to surrender themselves to Me so that I may transform them, for them to surrender their humanity to Me so that I may work in the world! Why do you not hear My call? Have I not exhausted every means to beg for your attention and your gratitude?" *(M.T., no. 231).*

"The best work that you can do is to obtain My cooperation—and, when you yourself have done all you could, to let Me act. I work with time. But My gifts are without regret." *(M.T., no. 276).*

"The purpose of your life does not lie in the personal merit due to your generosity; your merit will lie in using all your generosity to allow Me to live in you." *(M.T., no. 328).*

"Remember this: the value of your existence is not in what you have done, or said, or suffered: it is in the part of your being that you have given to your Saviour; in what you have allowed Me to do with you. Give Me your heart—and your heart is your whole life!" *(M.T., no. 349).*

"It is the sun that gives the earth its beauty and animates it. It is My grace that gives souls their beauty and that animates them. My Omnipotence is limited only by your liberty. It is with coal that I make diamonds. What would I not do with a soul, however black she might be, who would give herself to Me." *(M.T., no. 559).*

"All souls could rapidly attain to the plenitude of their sanctity if they allowed Me to act, without resisting. Oh, the unacknowledged reserves of selfishness which paralyze the omnipotence of the Holy Spirit within you!" *(M.T., no. 608).*

"Most religious give Me their work and their talents—I have sufficient talents at My disposal; what I desire is the *soul,* to make it My place of rest and of work, to live anew in it in humanity. Yes, My place of work, because a soul that would give herself to Me without reserve, how I would use her for the glory of God and of the Church, for the salvation of other souls, to a degree that you cannot imagine!" *(M.T., no. 380).*

"The best gift that you can make Me is to receive Me." *(M.T., no. 525).*

"Yes, I can transform all ugliness into beauty—all poverty into spiritual wealth—all sin into a source of grace—all rancor into forgiveness—into sweetness all bitterness—into joy all sadness—all suffering into Redemption . . . when you give them to Me and let Me act . . ." *(M.T., no. 313).*

~3~

CHARITY TOWARD OUR NEIGHBOR

"The Communion of Saints, fellowship, brotherly mutual
help are gifts of God. The human means given you, use
them." *(M.T., no. 248)*.

"Your Sister's wish is My wish." *(M.T., no. 255)*.

"No soul will enter My paradise without having forgiven at
least once." *(M.T., no. 309)*.

[Applied to fraternal charity]: "Why are you not content
with what the Church says? 'He who is not against Me is
with Me.'" *(M.T., no. 578)*.

"A true mother will not consider her child ugly, no matter
how much it may be so; to her it is always lovely, and so it
will always remain in her innermost heart. That is precisely
the way My Heart feels toward souls: though they be ugly,
soiled, filthy, My love considers them always beautiful. I
suffer when their ugliness is confirmed to Me; on the other
hand, I rejoice when, in conformity with My parental
sentiments, someone dissuades Me about their ugliness and
tells Me that it is not true and that they are still beautiful.
The souls are Mine; for them I have given all My Blood!

"Now do you understand how much My parental Heart is
wounded by every severe judgment, reprimand, or
condemnation, even though based on truth, and how much
comfort, on the other hand, is afforded Me by every act of
compassion, indulgence and mercy? You must never judge
anyone; never say a harsh word against anyone; instead,
console My Heart, distract Me from My sorrow; with eager
charity make Me see only the good side of a guilty soul. I
will believe you, and then I will hear your prayer in her favor
and will grant it. If you only knew how I suffer when I must
dispense justice! You see, My Heart needs to be comforted; It

7

wishes to dispense mercy , not justice!" *(C.B., p.40-41)*.

"I cherish each soul with a tenderness of which your human love has no conception. Do you not understand that? They must be loved for My sake. Strive to make it known to all whom I put in your path." *(M.T., no. 178)*.

"There is not a single material advantage, however great it may be, that ought not to be sacrificed to charity, or that justifies actions against charity." *(M.T., no. 357)*.

"Material misfortunes can always be remedied, and they affect only things that are destined to pass away." *(M.T., no. 357)*.

"To act against charity is an incalculable misfortune, difficult to repair because the consequences live on—and it is depriving God, for all eternity, of a homage that should have been paid to Him—for every act of charity honors God and makes Him known, and makes Him loved." *(M.T., no. 357)*.

"You hinder the flowering of My life in your Sisters' souls when you cause them some displeasure or vexation: yes, it is I who suffer through it. In order that I may grow in souls, I need them to be at ease, without bitterness, in kind dispositions—and how can one make others good . . . except by lavishing kindness on them . . .?" *(M.T., no. 449)*.

"It is I, your Jesus, whom you love in your neighbor; I, who am hidden in each soul, that I may grow there, I have such need to meet a heart that desires Me there and loves Me . . ." *(M.T., no. 17)*.

"These are two very different things: when you are kind to a soul whom, at the bottom of your heart, you do not esteem; or when you use your kindness to seek and find the beauty hidden in a soul that you are not inclined to esteem." *(M.T., no. 128)*.

"I need to see all of you happy in My service. Seek to give your Sisters what will give them pleasure and what they desire, and not what it pleases you to give." *(M.T., no. 239)*.

"Your neighbor is always I, I who am asking of you or giving to you. The Holy Trinity is there in his soul. And if It has been driven out by sin, help your neighbor to receive It back by treating him as if I were already dwelling within him." *(M.T., no. 143).*

"When I say that you must forgive one another, it is not a duty that I impose on you—can one impose love? It is a joy that I offer you; it is a share in My way of acting, a share in My Spirit . . ." *(M.T., no. 323).*

"I am in the Holy Eucharist—I am in you and in your Sisters. Each time you approach one of your Sisters, you meet Me anew, you renew your Communion with Me. What more could you want . . .?" *(M.T., no. 347).*

"It is wrong to believe that one spoils souls and characters by too much kindness and by yielding to all their wishes. Kindness is the most powerful aid. It is absolutely necessary that you should be kind one towards another, that you should do to others what you would wish them to do to you. One spoils souls by concealing from them what God requires of them, His demands and His beauty. One spoils souls by hiding God from them." *(M.T., no. 216).*

"Be charitable, above all in your *thoughts:* the rest will follow spontaneously of itself." *(M.T., no. 389).*

"It is impossible for you to know the value and the virtue of others, but you will never have too great a respect for souls, because I have redeemed them all at the price of My Blood." *(M.T., no. 582).*

"When you are united among yourselves, you can obtain everything from God, because you have obtained from yourselves the most difficult thing. And I have the joy of giving rewards . . ." *(M.T., no. 436).*

"Each time that by kindness in word or deed you encourage good understanding between you—mutual support and help—you contribute to the *unity* of My Church: 'That they may all be one.'" *(M.T., no. 232).*

"It is necessary for your mind to open itself to other minds in order to communicate with them, and also in order to receive the words of those who are My servants, above all of My priests, who pass on My doctrine, who speak as My 'other selves.'" *(M.T., no. 248).*

"The greatest charity you can show to your neighbor is to live in the silence of the cloister and in the effacement of your own nature—letting Me work through you. Then you are united to My action: you and I make but one—and I do not wound souls when I draw near to them." *(M.T., no. 575).*

"My little daughter, it is a small matter to be kind to those who are kind to you—but to be kind, very kind— for love of Me, to those who make you suffer, is really to belong to My family." *(M.T., no. 627).*

"The difficulties that arise among you, suspicions, misunderstandings, jealousies, or whatever they may be, are the pieces of wood that must feed the fire of fraternal love; do you not feel, after every reconciliation, that your love has grown, that it is stronger than before? Each time that one of these difficulties arises, My little daughter, think of its purpose: reconciliation—and let your heart be filled with hope!" *(M.T., no. 630).*

CHOSEN SOULS

"My Heart is never wounded unless it be by My chosen souls." *(J.M., p.72).*

"If their infidelities wound Me deeply, their love consoles and delights My Heart to such a degree that I, so to speak, forget the sins of many others on their account." *(J.M., p.250).*

"I rest in your nothingness, but I find comfort and relief as well in the midst of My consecrated nuns, for though they are unaware of it, I entrust them too with souls who are saved and return to Me." *(J.M., p.260).*

"O chosen souls, your happiness and perfection do not lie in following your attraction . . . but only and solely in embracing with love God's will, and being in perfect conformity with it in all it requires of you for His glory and your holiness." *(J.M., p.285-286).*

"You came to the convent for Me; nevertheless after a time I am the last in your thoughts. My help is asked, yes, but it is seldom that My wishes are consulted, and that I am listened to. I am given what it pleases you to give Me; it appears as if it would be time wasted to find out whether it is what I ask and desire. And yet that is the first thing that must fill your time." *(M.T., no. 256).*

"To become one of My religious is not to choose for oneself a lodging and livelihood like those who remain in the world— or a profession according to one's ability. It is something much more important, much greater. Oh, if everyone could understand that! It is to pledge oneself to live . . . My humble and hidden life, My life so penitential through its toil, and through its poverty and simplicity, My courageous and vigilant life, My redemptive life." *(M.T., no. 254).*

"There are many souls in the world who give Me what those who are officially and openly My Spouses refuse Me. If they do not espouse My desires, nor My tastes, nor My Cross—the Cross which I send them—nor My crown of thorns, nor the humiliations that I would send them if they were willing to receive them—are they really My Spouses?" *(M.T., no. 267)*.

"Most souls are anxious above all to go to Heaven and to escape Hell. I wish My Spouses to be less anxious about going to Heaven than about occupying there the place I have prepared for them: that is to say, to correspond in every way to My desires. As for My call to follow Me, many put it on as a servant's uniform while keeping their own desires at the bottom of their hearts. How few work to know My desires and to fulfill them!" *(M.T., no. 336)*.

"Did you enter the religious life in order that I might fulfill your wishes or in order that you might strive to fulfill Mine? . . ." *(M.T., no. 339)*.

"The religious life is so great a thing that even if a postulant were to die after only a few days of postulancy, she would have for all eternity a degree of charity far greater than if she had stayed in the world; only a few days separate her from the world, but already in her soul, an abyss separates her, because she has made that interior act of giving Me her liberty." *(M.T., no. 433)*.

"It is the religious who is the poorest, the most stripped through love, she who has nothing more to give, who gives most to the Community—because she lives closer to her Rule and to Me." *(M.T., no. 527)*.

"My little daughter, your time, your Holy Rule, your vows no longer belong to you. I gave them to you because you wished to consecrate them to Me. You have no right to live them according to your fancy; you must live them according to the spirit of the Church. The Church is I." *(M.T., no. 652)*.

"I ask three things of My consecrated souls: Reparation . . . Love . . . Confidence . . ." *(J.M., p.427)*.

~ 5 ~

CONFIDENCE

"I make little account of all that [miseries and weakness], provided souls come to Me with confidence and love. I Myself make up for all their frailty." *(J.M., p.133).*

"Have no fears, for your shortcomings are repaired by My Heart, and so are those of all souls. But the one thing that I ask is that they should not fail in trust, since I am their Saviour and their Spouse." *(J.M., p.192, 1st ed.).*

"Why fear? I am your Saviour and Bridegroom. If only souls understood all these two words imply." *(J.M., p.171).*

"It is the same when they pray, either for themselves or for others; if they waver and doubt, they do not glorify My Heart, but they do glorify It if they are sure that I will give them what they ask, knowing that I refuse them nothing that is good for their souls." *(J.M., p.422).*

"Weakness and worthlessness are of small account; what I want is their trust. These are the souls who draw down on the world mercy and peace." *(J.M., p.189).*

"I can refuse nothing to one who relies entirely on Me. Souls are too little conscious of how much I want to help them and how much I am glorified by their trust." *(J.M., p.327).*

"Let them [souls] give themselves up to thoughts of confidence, not fear, for I am a God of pity, ever ready to receive them into My Heart." *(J.M., p.244).*

"When you have all that is necessary, you deprive Me of the joy of taking care of you." *(M.T., no. 1).*

"Let Me have the pleasure of defending you at the right time." *(M.T., no. 2).*

13

"It is My joy to respond as God to humble confidence."
(M.T., no. 11).

"You must do *all* that you can, and it is only after that, that you can count infallibly on My help." *(M.T., no. 84).*

"You honor Me more by the confidence you show Me than by all that you could give Me." *(M.T., no. 95).*

"To those who ask with love, that is to say, with unlimited confidence, I cannot prevent Myself from granting even more, far more than what is asked." *(M.T., no. 215).*

"To love Me is to have confidence in Me, not to doubt Me; it is to rely on Me. Wherein lies the limit of My power over you? In your confidence." *(M.T., no. 237).*

"Go on with the strength that I give you, without worrying about how much you have." *(M.T., no. 623).*

"Oh, if you knew what My love is! And how I long for you to have confidence in it!" *(M.T., no. 88).*

"You see, even in good thoughts which creep in, there is always a bit of self-love, of complacency; and it is easy to see how they will spoil the act of love. But if you will have complete trust in Me, that I am attending to everything and will continue to do so, and if you will not permit even one other thought to enter, then your act of love will possess a virginal purity." *(C.B., p.144-145).*

"Consolata, place no limits on your confidence in Me, then I will place no limits on My graces for you!" *(C.B., p.59).*

"Trust always in Jesus! If you only knew how much pleasure that gives Me! Grant Me this solace to trust in Me even in the shadow of death." *(C.B., p.60).*

"You will be lacking in help only when My Divine Heart will be lacking in power." *(Our Lord to St. Margaret Mary).*

"Consolata, it often happens that good and pious souls, and very frequently also souls who are consecrated to Me, wound

14

My Heart to Its very depths by some diffident phrase such as: 'Who knows whether I will be saved?'

"Open the Gospel and read there My promises. I promised to My sheep: 'I will give them life everlasting; and they shall not perish forever, and no man shall pluck them out of My Hand.' Do you understand, Consolata? No one can take a soul from Me! Now read on: 'That which My Father hath given Me, is greater than all; and no one can snatch them out of the Hand of My Father.' Do you understand, Consolata? No one can snatch a soul from Me. . . . In all eternity they will not perish . . . because I give them eternal life. For whom have I spoken these words? For all the sheep, for all souls! Why then the insult, 'Who knows whether I will be saved?' I have given assurances in the Gospel that no one can pluck a soul from Me and that I will give that soul eternal life, and so the soul cannot perish. Believe Me, Consolata, into Hell go only those who really wish to go there; for though no one can snatch a soul from Me, the soul may, through the free will granted her, flee from Me, may betray Me, deny Me, and so go to Satan of her own volition.

"Oh, if instead of wounding My Heart with such distrust, you would give a little thought to the Heaven which awaits you! I did not create you for Hell but for Heaven, not as a companion for the devil but to enjoy Me in everlasting love! You see, Consolata, to Hell go only those who wish to go there. . . . How foolish is your fear of being damned! After having shed My Blood in order to save your soul, after having surrounded your soul with graces upon graces all through your entire existence . . . would I permit Satan, My worst enemy, to rob Me of that soul at the last moment of her life, just when I am about to gather in the fruit of the Redemption and when therefore that soul is on the point of loving Me forever? Would I do that, when in the Holy Gospel I have promised to give the soul eternal life and that no one can snatch her from My Hands? Consolata, how is it possible to believe such a monstrosity? You see, final impenitence is found only in a soul who purposely wishes to go to Hell and therefore obstinately refuses My mercy, for I never refuse to pardon anyone. I offer the gift of My immense compassion to all, for My Blood was shed for all, for all! No, it is not the multiplicity of sins which condemns a soul, for I forgive

15

everything if she repents, but it is the obstinacy of not wishing to be pardoned, of wishing to be damned! Dismas on the cross had only one single act of faith in Me, but many, many sins; he was pardoned in an instant, however, and on the very day of his repentance he entered into My kingdom and is a saint! Behold the triumph of My Mercy and of faith in Me!

"No, Consolata, My Father who has given Me the souls is greater and more powerful than all the demons. No one can snatch souls from the Hand of My Father!

"O Consolata, have confidence in Me! Trust Me always! You must have a blind confidence that I will fulfill all the great promises which I have made you, for I am kind, immensely kind and merciful, and 'I desire not the death of the wicked, but that the wicked turn from his way, and live.'" *(C.B., p.42-44).*

"It is My joy to give you hour by hour sufficient strength, to have you entirely dependent on My love." *(M.T., no. 364).*

"The future is Mine, what do you fear?" *(M.T., no. 9).*

"Let go of all that is not necessary to you—all that does not lead you directly to Me, so as to be altogether Mine." *(M.T., no. 11).*

"Love Me, and don't be afraid of your weakness, for I will sustain you. You love Me and I love you, you are Mine and I am yours. What more do you want?" *(J.M., p.221).*

"When a soul asks of Me what to human eyes is impossible, she honors Me. You are in fact asking Me for that which one asks only of God." *(M.T., no. 276).*

"Consolata, you must never, never, never commit that fault of doubting that I would keep My promises because of your unfaithfulness! Promise Me that, won't you? Do not offer Me that insult, for you would cause Me great suffering!" *(C.B., p.52).*

"This is the only reality: *I love you and I take care of you.*

16

And that is for now and for eternity." *(M.T., no. 5)*.

"It is not sufficient to say: 'My God, I have confidence in You.' You must make the interior act of freeing yourself from all anxiety, and rest on My Heart . . . like St. John, the Beloved Apostle. I await this confidence from every soul." *(M.T., no. 125)*.

"It is not what you give Me that glorifies Me; it is when, by your confidence, you give Me the opportunity of showing you what My love is capable of devising for you . . ." *(M.T., no. 161)*.

"Not one of those who have trusted in Me has ever been disappointed. My little daughter, you would be the first to whom that would happen: why do you doubt?" *(M.T., no. 432)*.

"When your Sisters have doubts concerning the help that you offer them, do you not feel that it paralyzes your spontaneity? It is the same with Me, because you are created in My likeness." *(M.T., no. 252)*.

"Rely on Me with closed eyes, without anxiety, content . . . yes, like a babe sleeping in its mother's arms. Are you not like babes carried in the arms of God?" *(M.T., no. 265)*.

DISTRACTIONS

"You see, Consolata, thoughts which come to you without your desiring them, do not make for unfaithfulness." *(C.B., p.83).*

"I leave you in the struggle against useless thoughts, for it is meritorious for you." *(C.B., p.83).*

"Do you desire the useless thoughts? No. Then everything is to your merit. When one desires only to love, then everything that obstructs that love becomes meritorious. Do you understand?" *(C.B., p.83).*

"I permit this assailing battle of thoughts which oppresses you, because it glorifies Me and gives Me souls. Offer Me these undesired thoughts at every instant with this ejaculation: 'For Thee and for souls!' I will transform these thoughts which come to you from morning to night, and which hinder your love, into graces and blessings for souls." *(C.B., p.83-84).*

"The act of love is like a train traveling along on its track; but if the track is cluttered up with useless thoughts, then the train cannot go on but must come to a stop. You see then how necessary the immaculate purity of mind is for you! So, not another thought, not even one! But what peace results from this, Consolata, is it not true? I alone must be in your mind!" *(C.B., p.137).*

"What is it that keeps you from loving Me, Consolata? It is useless thoughts and being interested in others! Consolata, if, while you are contemplating the sky, you let your eyes rest on the windows of the neighboring houses, you will find death. Similarly, if, instead of loving Me alone, you rest your eyes on the actions of others, you will find death!" *(C.B., p.90-91).*

"When phantoms pass before your mind, it matters little to you whether they come from your imagination, or from a good or bad spirit; use them by praying for what is presented to you." *(M.T., no. 181)*.

"Do not allow yourself to become engrossed in your little occupations; they are secondary. They are for your fingers; they are not to monopolize all your thoughts. You remain near Me, but your mind is saturated with mere nothings! It is as if you fell asleep at My Feet while My Heart was calling you." *(M.T., no. 245)*.

7

FAITH

[Josefa]: "The more they [souls] have lived in the obscurity of faith, the more Jesus will help them and reward them at the hour of death." *(J.M., p.446)*.

"Do you know what draws Me to your soul? It is the blind faith which you have in Me! The blind, childlike, limitless faith which you have in Me, pleases me greatly, and it is on that account that I bend down to you with so much love and with such tenderness." *(C.B., p.58)*.

"Pray that faith may spread. It transforms everything. Do you understand what is the greatest act of love that you can offer Me? It is when you make an act of pure faith. Faith places you in the light of that order in which you were created. You must follow that light." *(M.T., no. 424)*.

"In the same way, Faith depends on your will. He who wishes to believe, receives Faith. No one else can make in his stead the act of will that will introduce Faith into his soul. Then Faith grows, it is stronger than your will; it takes possession of the soul, which can no longer do without it. Without Faith you wander like sheep without a shepherd." *(M.T., no. 204)*.

"I hide My Divinity—I hide My Glory—I hide My power: the sight of them would crush you. And I am more honored and pleased to see that in spite of everything you believe in Me." *(M.T., no. 298)*.

"Now you must live by Faith; you must believe that I am there under the humble species, believe without proof. You must believe without proof that I use your sacrifices, your prayers, all your sufferings for the salvation of souls." *(M.T., no. 594)*.

"The faith of those who believe because they have seen a miracle has no root within themselves; it attests the miracle, it does not glorify Me—another miracle might efface it. The faith of those who believe without having seen has its roots within themselves, in their free will which they direct towards Me to glorify Me. Their faith honors Me." *(M.T., no. 443).*

"Faith is also a form of obedience: the submission of the mind." *(M.T., no. 299).*

"The greatest proof of love that you can give Me is to believe in Me." *(M.T., no. 588).*

8

FAULTS AND THEIR USE

"You must not grieve overmuch at your falls. Why, I could make a saint of you without more ado . . ." *(J.M., p.52-53)*.

[Mary:] "If you fall, do not be afflicted above measure. We are both here to raise you up, and I will never forsake you." *(J.M., p.60)*.

[Josefa:] "The more I see how kind He is, the worse I feel about myself. Drawing me gently to His Heart, He said: 'When a tiny child turns its back on his father, do you think he takes offense? . . . Come, rest in My Heart.'" *(J.M., 1st ed., p.64-65)*.

"If you should happen to commit some fault, do not grieve over it, but come and place it quickly within My heart; then strengthen your determination to strive for the opposite virtue, but with great calmness. In that manner your every fault will become a step in advance." *(C.B., p.49)*.

"A soul will profit even after the greatest sins, if she humbles herself." *(J.M., p.104)*.

"I will raise up the humble, and make little of their frailties, and even of their falls, provided they have humility and love." *(J.M., p.104)*.

"I left you to yourself, Josefa, that you might see how little you can do without Me . . . now do not think of it any more. Take My Cross, and let us go together to labor for souls." *(J.M., 1st ed., p.125)*.

"Even your falls comfort Me. Do not be discouraged, for this act of humility which your fault drew from you has consoled Me more than if you had not fallen." *(J.M., p.252-253)*.

"In spite of its miseries, a soul can love Me to folly ... But Josefa, you must realize that I am speaking only of faults of frailty and inadvertence, not of willed sin or voluntary infidelity." *(J.M., p.202)*.

"Listen, Consolata, if the good thief, in addition to all his own, had also committed all your faults, do you suppose I would have changed My verdict?" [Consolata:] "Oh no, Jesus, Thou wouldst have said just the same: 'Today thou shalt be with Me in paradise!'" [Jesus:] "Well then, some evening I will say the same words to you!" *(C.B., p.47)*.

"Look, Consolata, your poverty is limited, but My love has no limits!" *(C.B., p.49)*.

"Never go to rest at night with the slightest shadow obscuring your soul. This I recommend to you with great insistence. When you commit a fault, repair it at once. I wish your soul to be as pure as crystal. Do not let your falls, however many, trouble you. It is trouble and worry that keep a soul from God." *(J.M., p.112)*.

"Do you not know, Josefa, that the more wretched souls are, the more I love them! ... If amongst all others *you* have won My Heart, it is on account of your littleness and misery." *(J.M., p.201)*.

"What I want them [chosen souls] to realize is that I love them more tenderly still, if after their weakness and falls they throw themselves humbly into My Heart; then I pardon them ... and I love them still." *(J.M., p.201)*.

"Those whose generosity is not equal to these daily endeavors and sacrifices will see their lives go by full only of promise which never comes to fruition. But in this, distinguish: to souls who habitually promise and yet do no violence to themselves nor prove their abnegation and love in any way, I say: 'Beware lest all this straw and stubble which you have gathered into your barns take fire or be scattered in an instant by the wind!' But there are others, and it is of them I now speak, who begin their day with a very good will and desire to prove their love. They pledge themselves to self-denial or generosity in this or that circumstance ... But when the time comes they are prevented by self-love, temperament, health, or I know not what from carrying out what a few hours before they quite sincerely purposed to do. Nevertheless they speedily acknowledge their weakness and, filled with shame, beg for pardon, humble themselves, and renew their promise . . . Ah! Let them know that these souls please Me as much as if they had nothing with which to reproach themselves." *(J.M., p.218-219)*.

"I do not say that by the fact of My choice, a [chosen] soul is freed from her faults and wretchedness. That soul may and will fall often again, but if she humbles herself, if she recognizes her nothingness, if she tries to repair her faults by little acts of generosity and love, if she confides and surrenders herself once more to My Heart . . . she gives Me more glory and can do more good to other souls than if she had never fallen. Miseries and weaknesses are of no consequence; what I do ask of them is love." *(J.M., p.201-202)*.

~9~

GENEROSITY

"When a soul is generous enough to give Me all I ask, she gathers up treasures for herself and others and snatches great numbers of souls from perdition." *(J.M., p.201)*.

"The more you give Me, the more will I increase your capacity for giving." *(M.T., no. 40)*.

"Do not lose a moment, not a single occasion of offering to Me all that I send you." *(M.T., no. 7)*.

"I am given what it pleases you [religious] to give Me; it appears as if it would be time wasted to find out whether it is what I ask and desire. And yet that is the first thing that must fill your time." *(M.T., no. 256)*.

"It is when a soul forgives and is silent that she most resembles My Mother." *(M.T., no. 259)*.

"As a rule, to do a little more than is required is to offer Me the perfume with the flower. This little extra effort, being voluntary, can only be an expression of love; it is more precious than all the rest; and usually it is neither seen nor known by anyone." *(M.T., no. 213)*.

"Most souls do not give their measure of generosity and love because no one asks it of them. It must be asked of them without being exacted; but it must be asked for, asked for on My behalf... When it is for Me, souls give; they do not refuse; they give even more than is asked of them." *(M.T., no. 180)*.

"I suffered much in My Passion, much more than was strictly necessary, but there was a reason for that excess of suffering. Therefore let there be no limit to your generosity; it is that which will feed your love and increase your

25

strength, it is that which will unfailingly draw down My gifts, because I am never outdone by generosity." *(M.T., no. 249)*.

"One must be blindly generous. Children must be taught generosity; it will turn their souls towards Me for the whole of their lives. Teach them to do rather more than not enough—to give always a little more than is actually asked of them. And in giving to hide their gifts." *(M.T., no. 249)*.

"There are sacrifices which I desire, but for which I do not ask—so as to leave to souls the joy of offering them to Me of themselves." *(M.T., no. 289)*.

"It is faith that gives generosity. Ask My Father—your Father—to increase your Faith and to spread it in the world." *(M.T., no. 393)*.

"If you wish to do something for Me, you must do over and above what is allowed, what is normal; yes, even to the folly of humiliation and of the Cross. A love that does not exaggerate is not love, it is affection." *(M.T., no. 544)*.

"You are astonished that often an effort that seemed impossible to make, instead of exhausting, strengthens you. It is not astonishing, it is true: I never allow Myself to be outdone by generosity ... Many souls deprive themselves of many graces because they refuse to make efforts which seem impossible to them, which are only offered to the generosity of their initiative." *(M.T., no. 557)*.

"My little daughter, to hit the target, good marksmen aim above it—they then hit it. Do you understand? To practice a virtue, do not be afraid of exaggerating that virtue—to attain to the love of the Cross, you must know the folly of the Cross." *(M.T., no. 625)*.

"All that the Father has, He has given to Me. Nothing is wanting to Me but your heart with its free will, which is yours. It is that which I ask of you." *(M.T., no. 153)*.

"Many souls exhaust themselves in efforts, in acts of generosity, which leave their soul bruised and impoverished, because they strain at an ideal of virtue, of sanctity that I do not ask of them. They will be rewarded for their pure intention and their generosity, but their efforts do not produce the fruit that they would produce if they were united to My will." *(M.T., no.555)*.

"Most religious give Me their work and their talents—I have sufficient talents at My disposal; what I desire is the *soul* to make it My place of rest and of work, to live anew in it, in humanity." *(M.T., no. 380)*.

10

HEAVEN

"The trials of your life on earth are such a small thing in comparison with that which they obtain for you for eternity." *(M.T., no. 287).*

"Ah, if you knew what a Friend you have in Heaven!" *(M.T., no. 459).*

"Celeste Canda is now enjoying the beatific vision for all eternity, and from Heaven she is watching over the souls of her four children with greater tenderness than if she had remained on earth." *(C.B., p.35).*

"You think you do not deserve these joys in eternity because you are doing nothing? Tell Me, what does the catechism say? That you have been created to love Me, serve Me, and to be happy with Me in all eternity. And you, do you not love Me? Do you not serve Me? Well, then you are entitled to the glory and joy of Heaven! I give you Heaven not only out of love, but out of justice." *(C.B., p.110).*

"Rejoice, My beloved! Are you not in a hurry to join Me? . . . I long to keep you near Me; I long for you to finish your preparation!" *(M.T., no. 136).*

"I wish every soul to understand that I am awaiting her. That beyond this life a boundless love awaits her, and that she must hasten . . . must purify herself to meet Love, and let that be her one object." *(M.T., no. 270).*

"If you only knew how great a thing it is: to appear before God. If the soul is ready, why wish to detain her? Think more of *her* than of yourselves." *(M.T., no. 319).*

"Most souls are anxious above all to go to Heaven and to escape Hell. I wish My Spouses to be less anxious about going to Heaven than about occupying there the place I have prepared for them: that is to say, to correspond in every way to My desires." *(M.T., no. 336).*

"But Josefa, do you not long to possess Me and enjoy Me without end? . . . I, on My part, long for you! I glory in those who do My will always and in all things, and for that reason I chose you. Leave Me free to do with you what I know will be both for My glory and for your good. The winter of this life is about to end. . . . I am your Beatitude." *(J.M., p.412).*

11

HOLINESS AND WHAT IT REQUIRES

[Josefa:] "How sad I feel that I cannot conquer myself nor correspond to so much goodness." [Jesus:] "Never mind. Cast yourself into My Heart, and follow the guidance that is given you. That will suffice." *(J.M., p.133).*

"I would like them [My chosen souls] to know how much I desire their perfection, and that it consists in doing their ordinary actions in intimate union with Me. If they once grasped this, they could divinize their life and all their activities by this close union with My heart . . . and how great is the value of a divinized day!" *(J.M., p.214).*

[Mary:] "Do not fear, my child, Jesus asks only for your good will." *(J.M., p. 225).*

[Josefa:] "Our Lord is so good, so kind when we do all we can, which of course is really nothing. He takes charge of the rest; it matters so little whether we feel we are getting better or not." *(J.M., p.448).*

"I ask nothing of them [religious and even all souls] that they do not possess. But I do ask that all they have they should give Me, for all is Mine. If they possess nothing but miseries and weakness, these I desire: even if they have only faults and sins, I desire them also. I beg them to give them to Me. Yes, give all to Me, keep nothing back, but trust My Heart. I forgive you, I love you, I will sanctify you Myself." *(J.M., p.unknown).*

"I so much want souls to understand this! It is not the action in itself that is of value; it is the intention with which it is done." *(J.M., p.213).*

"I want you to be holy, very holy, and you will only become so by the path of humility and obedience. . . ." *(J.M., p.111).*

"The more you give Me, the more I will increase your capacity for giving." *(M.T., no. 40).*

"It is not sins that injure your purity, it is your pride, which, so often, does not wish to acknowledge them." *(M.T., no. 582).*

"Love is sanctity. The more you love Me, the more you will become holy!" *(C.B., p.106).*

"You are too little to form intentions. I will decide the purpose of your life. Just love Me continually, and do not interrupt your act of love!" *(C.B., p.166).*

"If a creature of good will desires to love Me and to make of her life one single act of love from the moment of her rising until she falls asleep at night—from the heart, be it well understood—then I will perform incredible things for that soul. Write that down!" *(C.B., p.119).*

"Remember, Consolata, that I am kind; do not distort this fact! You see, the world likes to represent sanctity by pictures of austerities, flagellations, chains ... But it is not like that. If sacrifice and penance do enter into the life of a saint, they are not on that account the whole of his life. The saint, or the soul who gives herself to Me with generosity, is the most fortunate being on earth, for I am kind, altogether kind." *(C.B., p.74).*

"Never lose sight of the fact that the Jesus whom you behold dying on the Cross at the end of His mortal career, is the same Jesus who for thirty years shared the life which is common to all men, in the bosom of His own family; and He is the same Jesus who all during His three years' ministry sat down to table with men and joined in their banquets. And Jesus was holy, Consolata, the holiest of all men!" *(C.B., p.74).*

"I do love the fidelity with which you are keeping your promises, but I also love your confidence in My parental goodness, and it will please Me if you will make exceptions when there is real need for it. Remember, and never forget: Jesus is kind! Do not misrepresent Me!" *(C.B., p.74).*

"My little daughter, the Sisters who cannot bear the discomfort of the heat in order to remain longer with Me, have not much love. It is the test of being able to bear your human imperfections that reveals My saints. It is not in great things, but in certain details which reveal great love, that I recognize them." *(M.T., no. 597).*

"It is I who do all imperceptibly, gradually; you have only to give Me your soul, to give it without reserve and without resisting My desires. It is thus that every soul finds all she desires." *(M.T., no. 192).*

"Sanctity is to allow Me to live in you, and it is I who bring it to pass within you. It is to give Me your human nature so that I may live on among you." *(M.T., no. 407).*

HUMILITY

"He who never needs forgiveness is not the most happy, but rather he who has humbled himself many times." *(J.M., p.153).*

"You must not be troubled, Josefa. I want you to be nothing, that I may be All." *(J.M., p.342).*

"I see the very depths of souls, I see how they would please, console and glorify Me, and the act of humility they are obliged to make when they see themselves so feeble is solace and glory to My Heart." *(J.M., p.174).*

"To Josefa, begging for humility, Jesus said, 'I possess humility for your pride.'" *(J.M., p.52).*

"A soul will profit even after the greatest sins, if she humbles herself. It is pride that provokes My Father's wrath, and it is loathed by Him with infinite hatred." *(J.M., p. 104).*

"Try to make many acts of humility, Josefa, and do not count the cost. If you but knew how pleasing such acts are to Me." *(J.M., 1st ed., p.116).*

"The better you know what you are, the better you will know what I am." *(J.M., p.112).*

"Little still implies some being, but, Josefa, you are less than that, you are nothingness personified." *(J.M., p.173).*

"You are the echo of My voice, but if I be silent, what are you then?" *(J.M., p.217).*

[The devil cried with a yell of rage:] "There is no doubt about it: all those who reach highest sanctity have sunk deepest in humility." *(J.M., p.232).*

"With ruins, on ruins, I can build magnificently. It gives Me joy to use that which has humbled itself before Me, because My action is free." *(M.T., no. 278).*

"It is with coal that I make diamonds. What would I not do with a soul, however black she might be, who would give herself to Me!" *(M.T., no. 559).*

"It is not sins that injure your purity, it is your pride, which, so often, does not wish to acknowledge them." *(M.T., no. 582).*

"Never forget it is from your nothingness that My treasures will be poured forth." *(J.M., p.76).*

"But note that when that child begins to talk and someone asks him who made his lovely little dress, he will reply quite happily, 'My mamma,' and he will delight in possessing that dress and the admiration it calls forth. Do you notice the difference between great souls and little souls? The latter enjoy the virtues with which they feel themselves adorned because it is God who has bestowed them; but the former conceal them for fear that, having labored in pursuit of them, they might lose them through pride. Do you understand, Consolata? . . . That is why I tell everything to little souls; they deprive Me of nothing; they direct all praise, honor, and glory to Me alone." *(C.B., p.28).*

"Do you understand that you are *nothing?* Apart from Me you are nothing but rebellion, refusal, negation." *(M.T., no. 29).*

"Do you think that I will abandon you at the moment of death, you who are so miserable that you cannot live without Me . . .? As a mother embraces her newborn child, so will I enfold you in My love; because you are My tiny child, and I know that you cannot do without Me . . ." *(M.T., no. 145).*

"Yes, pride leads to a crashing fall, and humility leads to light and glory—yes, to the glory of God, the sight of which is enough to overfill your capacity for happiness. The happiness of God becomes the happiness of the humble soul." *(M.T., no. 350).*

"There are several forms of humility: that which admits your nothingness, your unworthiness, speaks according to wisdom and truth. But it is also a form of humility not to speak of oneself, because one does not think of oneself; one thinks only of Me. I love that silence concerning oneself . . ." *(M.T., no. 650).*

"I want them [My consecrated souls] to know that I love them as they are. I know that through frailty they will fall more than once. I know that they will often break the promises they have made Me. But their will to do better glorifies Me, their humble avowals after their falls, their trust in the forgiveness I will grant, glorify My Heart so much, that I will shed abundant graces on them." *(J.M., p.423).*

"Instead of developing your talents, seek rather to welcome the gifts of God, all His gifts; your souls will be loaded with imperishable riches." *(M.T., no. 248).*

"Comfort Me, you whom I love! It is because you are so little that you are able to creep so deeply into My Heart." *(J.M., p.203).*

"I do not say that by the fact of My choice, a soul is freed from her faults and wretchedness. That soul may and will fall often again, but if she humbles herself, if she recognizes her nothingness, if she tries to repair her faults by little acts of generosity and love, if she confides and surrenders herself once more to My Heart . . . she gives Me more glory and can do more good to other souls than if she had never fallen. Miseries and weaknesses are of no consequence, what I do ask of them is love." *(J.M., p.201-202).*

"When you do not think of yourself, My grace visits you, and I provide what is necessary for you. When you try to do it yourself, I leave you to your own care." *(M.T., no. 327).*

~ 13 ~

JESUS
Our All and Our Only Good

"What would you do if you had not My Heart? . . . But the more feeble you are, the more tenderly I love you." *(J.M., p.133).*

"Why fear? I am your Saviour and Bridegroom. If only souls understood all these two words imply." *(J.M., p.171).*

[If one is roused from a state of tepidity:] "Ah! Hasten to My Heart . . . You know that in your Superiors, whoever they may be . . . I am there concealed under the veil of faith . . . Lift the veil and tell Me all about your sufferings, miseries and falls with complete confidence." *(J.M., 1st ed., p.312).*

"I require nothing of you beyond what is already yours. Give Me an empty heart and I will fill it . . . give Me a heart destitute of all adornment and I will make it beautiful. Give it to Me with all its miseries, and I will consume them. What is hidden from you I will reveal, and all that you lack, I take on Myself to supply." *(J.M., p.346).*

"Have no fear about your wretchedness and misery, your carelessness or even your faults . . . I Myself will supply for all. My Heart is the Repairer par excellence." *(J.M., p.376-377).*

[Mary to Josefa:] "Little children have no acquired merits, and so it is with you. You are the beloved of His Heart without having done anything to merit it. He it is who does everything in you, who pardons you, who loves you." *(J.M., p.406).*

"Well do you say: 'Jesus, Josefa's all . . . Josefa, the misery of Jesus.'" *(J.M., 1st ed., p.328).*

"What does all the rest matter? . . . Your sins? Why, I can wipe them out . . . Your miseries? I consume them . . . Your weakness? I will be its support . . . Let us remain united." *(J.M., p.336).*

"Unceasingly use My Life, My Blood, My Heart . . . confide constantly and without any fear in this Heart: this secret is known to few; I want you to know it and to profit by it." *(J.M., p.405).*

"Your littleness has given place to My greatness . . . your misery, and even your sins, to My mercy . . . your trust to My love and tenderness." *(J.M., p.436).*

"Take this Heart and offer It to your God. By It, you can pay all your debts." *(J.M., p.96).*

"I am the great Victim, and you are a very little one, but if you are united to Me, My Father will listen to you." *(J.M., p.123).*

"My Heart is powerful enough to sustain you. It is yours; take from It all you need." *(J.M., p.136).*

[Mary:] "Do not regard your wretchedness, but look at the treasure that is yours, for if you are all His, He is all yours." *(J.M., p.172).*

"Josefa, since you are My bride, you know that it is your duty to comfort the Bridegroom . . . and the Bridegroom's part is to sustain and strengthen the bride." *(J.M., 1st ed., p.244).*

"Let Me enter into you, work at you, consume and destroy you, so that it is no longer your will that acts, but Mine." *(J.M., p.303).*

"The less there is of you, the more I shall be your life, and you will be My heaven of rest . . . on earth My heaven is in souls." *(J.M., p.343).*

"The more you disappear, the more shall I be your life. . . . My Heart is yours, take it and repair with it." *(J.M., p.181).*

"I know your wretchedness, Josefa, and I take on Myself to make reparation for it; you on your part, make reparation for souls." *(J.M., p.394).*

[Consolata:] "O Jesus, I am so worthless!" [Jesus:] "Then unite yourself to strength!" [Consolata:] "How can I do that?" [Jesus:] "By remaining in love. United to strength, you will be stronger than the strong!" *(C.B., p.108).*

"Now, what do you need in order to give Me this continual act of love? You need the twofold silence of thought and word toward everyone, and to see and treat Me in everyone. I will think through you, I will speak through you, I will write through you, but you must be intent solely on loving Me, and loving Me always! That should be your one and only thought from the time of your rising in the morning until you fall asleep at night." *(C.B., p.137).*

"I have been loving on your behalf, and so I count your entire day as one continuous act of love." *(C.B., p.30).*

"If you are in Me and we are one, then you will bring forth much fruit and will become strong, for you will disappear like a drop of water in the ocean; My silence will pass into you, and My humility, My purity, My charity, My gentleness, My patience, My thirst for suffering, and My zeal for souls whom I wish to save at all costs!" *(C.B., p.78-79).*

"Remember and keep it well fixed in your mind, you who long so much to gather abundant fruit: in the Gospels I did not declare that you would bring forth much fruit if you undertook extraordinary mortifications, but that you would do so if you remained in Me. Therefore, do not depart from the straight road, but devote your every effort to remaining well united with the Vine. Do not separate yourself from the thought of 'Jesus only!'—not even by a single thought or an uncalled-for word. I will think of everything!" *(C.B., p. 94).*

"Remain fixed in Me—like the little magnetized needle of the compass." *(M.T., no. 556).*

[Josefa:] "I asked Him how we can console Him, since we are so full of miseries and weakness. He answered me by pointing to His Heart: 'I make little account of all that, provided souls come to Me with confidence and love. I Myself make up for all their frailty.'" *(J.M., p.133)*.

"Love will despoil you of self and allow you to think only of My glory and of souls." *(J.M., p.96)*.

[Jesus to Sister Mary:] "There is only one reality: I love you. You are Mine." *(M.T., no. 513)*.

"I give fullness of joy to the soul who has really met Me and who receives Me. She then renounces all secondary things without pain, provided she may keep her God!" *(M.T., no. 111)*.

14

JOY

"I want you to be very little and very humble, and always gay." *(J.M., p.112).*

"Often choose what costs you, but without loss of joy and gladness, for by serving Me in peace and happiness you will give the most glory to My Heart." *(J.M., p.112).*

"Your joy is to strip yourselves and to be dependent on Me alone. My joy is to be able to prove to you the prodigality of My love." *(M.T., no. 126).*

"When I see those who love Me obey with difficulty, it humiliates Me; when prayer, when virtue costs them something, it humiliates Me; I who have said that My yoke is easy and My burden light! Serve Me with a heart that sings!" *(M.T., no. 219).*

"The joys that tomorrow will bring you are wrapped up in those of today; if you welcome those of the present, they will open your heart to those of tomorrow." *(M.T., no. 197).*

"I love you! Is that not enough to fill every one of your moments with the fullness of joy? I love you and desire that you should know it. Oh, if you knew how much I love you, My little child!" *(M.T., no. 55).*

"I would rather see a soul give Me little but with great joy, than see her give Me much, see her consecrate to Me all that a human life can consecrate, but with sadness; sadness is like a regret." *(M.T., no. 220).*

"Time that is filled with joy, with joy directed toward God, is not lost time." *(M.T., no. 208).*

"You have always the joy of being able to give; and the

poorest, those who have nothing to give, can still give their heart and their soul to God—that is the greatest gift: it embraces all others . . ." *(M.T., no. 295).*

"Yes, you are tired; but is it not your greatest joy to have something to offer Me? Or do I not know My little spouse. . . .?" *(M.T., no. 233).*

"I need to see all of you happy in My service. Seek to give your Sisters what will give them pleasure and what they desire, and not what it pleases you to give." *(M.T., no. 239).*

"My little daughter, serve Me with joy, give Me much joy—it bears witness to My Presence. I give to you, and you cannot offer Me anything better than My gifts; if you bring Me only pain and effort, you bring Me that which comes from yourself, and what have you done with the joy I sent you . . .?" *(M.T., no. 383).*

"I am always in a joyous heart. Sadness reigns where I have not been welcomed . . . joy of soul, which the world does not always see, is the first of all your messages to rise to Heaven." *(M.T., no. 383).*

"To bear monotony, the tediousness of the same work coming round regularly, the absence of novelty, while keeping a joyful heart, is to honor Me—that is to conform oneself to My hidden life. To be joyous simply because I am with you, when you have no other reason for being so, that is to prove to Me that you love Me . . ." *(M.T., no. 386).*

"Yes, there is more happiness in giving than in receiving. But do you know that there is also more happiness in letting oneself be stripped through love than in receiving? And more happiness in making reparation than in doing additional good work?" *(M.T., no. 483).*

"My beloved, I wish to fill you with joy! Humiliations, contempt, being forgotten by other creatures, these are the joys that I will give you." *(M.T., no. 501).*

"It is so: to be happy, one must give. You see quite well that each time you give, My joy echoes within you. Each time you

41

give, it is as if you took a step nearer Me." *(M.T., no. 548)*.

"You could be so happy! You have only to conform to what your Rule, which is Holy, and your Constitutions indicate to you. It is I who do all the rest." *(M.T., no. 662)*.

"Ah, if you understood! How happy each soul could be in My intimacy! The pettinesses that *blind* you would, of themselves, disappear in this ever-growing quest for Love. . . ." *(M.T., no. 169)*.

"Look at My Heart, Josefa. It alone can make you happy. Rest in It." *(J.M., p.34)*.

15

LOVE
God's Love for Us

"Ah! If only they [souls] knew My Heart . . . mankind is ignorant of Its mercy and goodness: that is My greatest sorrow." *(J.M., p.82)*.

"I have contracted an alliance of love and mercy with you. Does love ever grow weary or mercy come to an end?" *(J.M., p.123)*.

"Nothing, indeed, is wanting to My heavenly beatitude, which is infinite, but I yearn for souls. . . . I thirst for them, and want to save them." *(J.M., p.377)*.

"Yes, I love all souls, but with very special affection those who are the most weak and little." *(J.M., p.399)*.

"Ah, if souls only understood how ardently I desire to communicate Myself to them! But how few do understand . . . and how deeply this wounds My Heart." *(J.M., p.109)*.

"I am all love, and how then could I treat severely those I so love?" *(J.M., p.201)*.

"See My wounds [from the scourging]! Who has suffered for love of you as I have?" *(J.M., p.279)*.

"This is the only reality: *I love you and I take care of you.*" *(M.T., no. 5)*.

"I bought you at the price of My Blood, the Blood of God. That I might not condemn you, I allowed Myself to be condemned in your place." *(M.T., no. 177)*.

"My love for you is so great that it could not be better

expressed than through suffering." *(M.T., no. 61)*.

"There is only one reality: I love you. You are Mine." *(M.T., no. 513)*.

"Do not make Me out a God of rigor, whereas I am nought but a God of Love!" *(C.B., p.36)*.

"Write 'The Gentle Heart of Jesus'; for everyone knows that I am holy, but not all know that I am gentle!" *(C.B., p.36)*.

"As I am happy, yes, *happy* to show you the marks of My Passion—see how your God has loved you!—will you not also be happy to show Me the marks of your love . . .? Oh, if you knew how I long for you! Not to reproach you, but to overwhelm you with joy in showing you the marks of My love . . ." *(M.T., no. 96)*.

"As parents are happy in showing their love to their children, so it is My joy to make My love felt, to reveal it; I do it in a reserved manner, perceptible to those who are attentive to My Presence and who seek it; because I am Spirit, and in order that a soul should really find Me, she must have sought and discovered Me. Then she associates Me with her life and perceives that she had been seeking Me too far away." *(M.T., no. 190)*.

"Do you understand that after having loved you so much in My earthly life, I cannot stop loving you—My gifts are without regret—do you understand how ready I am to help you, to give you My grace? You can ask everything of Me; come to Me!" *(M.T., no. 425)*.

"Love gives Itself as food to Its own and this food is the substance which gives them their life and sustains them. Love humbles Itself before Its own . . . and in so doing raises them to the highest dignity. Love surrenders Itself in totality, It gives in profusion and without reserve. With enthusiasm, with vehemence It is sacrificed, It is immolated, It is given for those It loves. . . . The Holy Eucharist is love to the extreme of folly." *(J.M., p.305)*.

"I wish you to be entirely Mine. You are so miserable! You

have such need of Me! I will shelter you in the secret places of My Heart; you are My tiny child!" *(M.T., no. 54).*

"I love you! Is that not enough to fill every one of your moments with the fullness of joy? I love you and desire that you should know it. Oh, if you knew how much I love you, My little child!" *(M.T., no. 55).*

"Leave all. Let there no longer be anything else in the world for you but the love between you and Me." *(M.T., no. 58).*

"Oh, if you knew what My love is! And how I long for you to have confidence in it!" *(M.T., no. 88).*

"As a mother embraces her newborn child, so will I enfold you in My love; because you are My tiny child, and I know that you cannot do without Me..." *(M.T., no. 145).*

"It is My joy to help you! I can do great things for Eternity with a soul who unreservedly gives herself to Me, letting Me work in her; and each soul, each one, is called to that. I await each one to confide her special mission to her, and the secrets My love keeps for her." *(M.T., no. 173).*

"Ah, if you knew how the Holy Trinity watches over you! You are lost, carried in its solicitude as a child in the womb of its mother—and like that child you are unaware of your happiness." *(M.T., no. 240).*

"I have bought you at a great price: you are Mine in the immensity of Love." *(M.T., no. 410).*

"Ah, if you knew what a Friend you have in Heaven!" *(M.T., no. 459).*

"You are in God, in His Power, as leaves abandoned to a breath of wind." *(M.T., no. 550).*

"Give Me your heart—that heart which creatures do not know and which they slight; it is more than a universe to Me, because I love you." *(M.T., no. 551).*

"It is such a great thing to belong to Me! What does

anything else matter to you? Be full of joy at belonging to Me. I want you to be altogether Mine!" *(M.T., no. 46)*.

"Am I not enough for you? Is it not sufficient for you to know that your Jesus loves you?" *(M.T., no. 49)*.

"When a king espouses the daughter of a subject, he assumes the obligation of providing all that the new rank to which he has raised her requires." *(J.M., p.346)*.

"Behold the Heart that gives life to souls; the fire of this love is stronger than the indifference and ingratitude of men." *(J.M., p.135)*.

"Each soul is a matchless treasure to Me." *(M.T., no. 152)*.

"Do not fear. Do you not know that My Heart has only one desire: to consume your wretchedness and to consume you yourself. . . . I know you, and love you . . . and I shall never grow tired of you." *(J.M., p.390)*.

"I give Myself to all souls; but I have secrets to give each one that are for her alone, with her mission which is hers alone." *(M.T., no. 169)*.

"I wish each soul to understand that she has her special place in My Heart which awaits her; that her love is necessary to Me; and her cooperation necessary—that I need to see her happy and perfect—because I have loved her even to dying on the Cross for her—yes, each soul." *(M.T., no. 247)*.

LOVE
Our Love for God

"Just as I sacrificed Myself as a victim of love, so I want you to be a victim: love never refuses anything." *(J.M., p.27).*

"This Heart . . . I want you to rest in It as a child, to love It as a spouse, and to console It as a victim." *(J.M., p.32).*

"It does not matter that it [your heart] is small! I will expand it, but let it be all Mine." *(J.M., p.192).*

"When two people love one another, a very small lack of consideration in one of them is sufficient to wound the other. And so it is with My Heart. That is why I want those who aspire to intimacy with Me to train themselves well so that later on they refuse Me nothing." *(J.M., p.203).*

[Mary:] "O! If only souls but knew Him better, they would love Him so much more." *(J.M., p.322).*

"To love Me is to have confidence in Me, not to doubt Me: it is to rely on Me. Wherein lies the limit of My power over you? In your confidence." *(M.T., no. 237).*

"The greatest proof of love that you can give Me is to believe in Me." *(M.T., no. 588).*

"I ask only for love. Ah, what are you doing about it . . .?" *(M.T., no. 44).*

"The best gift that you can make Me is to receive Me." *(M.T., no. 525).*

"Love is good actions freely performed. I never refuse love to someone who asks for it—but it is your will, your actions that will develop it in you." *(M.T., no. 204).*

"When two love one another as Bride and Bridegroom, if one suffers, so does the other." *(J.M., 1st ed., p.70).*

"Write this down, Consolata—for I demand it of you under obedience—that for one act of love from you I would create Heaven!" *(C.B., p.67).*

"I prefer an act of love and a Communion of love to any other gift . . . I thirst for love." *(C.B., p.75).*

"Love Me, and you will be happy; and the more you love Me, the happier you will be! Even when you will find yourself in utter darkness, love will produce light, love will produce strength, and love will produce joy!" *(C.B., p.106-107).*

"Oh, if people would only love Me, what felicity would reign in this unhappy world!" *(C.B., p.107).*

"Consolata, you know that I love you very much! My Heart is divine, yes, but It is also human like yours; and so It longs for your love, for your every thought . . . I shall take care of everything, even the most trivial matters, but you must think only of Me!" *(C.B., p.81).*

"Love Me alone! I will attend to maintaining you in humility. If you will but dwell in Me, that which is in the vine will also be in the branches." *(C.B., p.105).*

"Your actions will have more value in proportion as you increase in love!" *(C.B., p.98).*

"Transform everything disagreeable that you meet with into little roses; gather them with love and offer them to Me with love." *(C.B., p.99).*

"I delight in gifts which are offered with all possible love. Then even your trifles become precious to Me." *(C.B., p.99).*

"No, Consolata, no! Jesus does not demand heroic acts from you, but merely trifles, only they must be offered with all your heart!" *(C.B., p.99).*

"When the heart is very sick, it makes even a robust person

inactive. Thus, if the heart does not belong to Me, I do not know what to make of the soul, no matter how much she is adorned with virtues." *(C.B., p.100).*

"That soul is dearest to Me who loves Me the most!" *(C.B., p.100).*

"Love Me, Consolata, love Me alone! Love is everything, and so you will be giving Me everything. When you love Me, you give Jesus everything He desires from His creature: love! Love is everything! If you will now concentrate upon this one resolution, you will be giving everything to Jesus!" *(C.B., p.97).*

"You see, Consolata, My creatures make Me out as one who is fear-inspiring rather than kind; and I, on the other hand, delight in being always and solely kind. What is it that I require? Love, and love only, for he who loves Me, serves Me." *(C.B., p.97).*

"You see, I long to have My creatures serve Me out of love. Therefore, if a soul avoids some fault for fear of My chastisements, that is not what I am longing for from My creatures. I desire to be loved; I crave the love of My creatures! When they will come to love Me, they will no longer offend Me. When two people really love each other, they never offend each other. That is precisely the way it ought to be between the Creator and His creatures." *(C.B., p.98).*

"They [chosen souls] need do nothing extraordinary to attain to a high degree of love." *(J.M., p.215).*

"Rather than with diligence, you should strive to do everything with much love. Whether you are working, eating, drinking, or sleeping, do everything with a great deal of love, for I thirst for love. Love is what I look for in every work." *(C.B., p.98).*

"Fix all your attention upon your task of the moment so as to accomplish it with all possible love." *(C.B., p.98).*

"Live by loving, one minute at a time! An entire day is too

49

long for you!" *(C.B., p.126)*.

"Do not leave Me, My poor little creature. If you knew how much you need Me! And I seek a heart whose love for Me is boundless." *(M.T., no. 18)*.

"Yes, I am love. You drive Me away every time that you act otherwise than love would suggest; and you deprive yourself of the power to love. Without Me your heart cannot love." *(M.T., no. 22)*.

"As those who are in love fix a meeting place during the day where they devote themselves solely to each other, so have we our meeting places: they are the Offices of the day and night, Mass, Holy Communion . . ." *(M.T., no. 118)*.

"Love does not keep for itself those whom it loves, it gives them away . . . One must love, to be able to give—so that the Holy Spirit may triumph and spread . . . As you need to feel yourselves loved so that you may blossom and open out to life, so do I need to feel Myself loved by you so that I may send you My gifts." *(M.T., no. 237)*.

"I am not known, and because I am not known, people do not know how to love Me, I who have so loved men." *(M.T., no. 361)*.

"For the more you know and love Me, the closer will you be united to all those who love Me. I do not separate the hearts that receive Me: I am union. And it is your love for Me that unites human hearts for eternity." *(M.T., no. 148)*.

"Time filled with love is time well filled. Love multiplies time. He who loves finds means of doing many things from the outpouring of his heart. Try today . . ." *(M.T., no. 257)*.

"If you knew how I need to find souls who love Me, who have used their day in preparing to receive Me! If you knew! You would prepare your soul better." *(M.T., no. 521)*.

"A love that does not exaggerate is not love, it is affection." *(M.T., no. 544)*.

"I want to tell you this, that My best-loved and specially favored souls, My priests and My consecrated nuns, may learn it through you. If their infidelities wound Me deeply, their love consoles and delights My Heart to such a degree that I, so to speak, forget the sins of many others on their account." *(J.M., p.250).*

"When souls are unable to remain long hours in My presence as they would like to, either because they must take their rest or go to preoccupying work which takes up all their attention, there is nothing to prevent their making a convention with Me, for when love is ingenious it can prove its worth in this way even more than by the ardor of its devotion when free and tranquil." *(J.M., p.296).*

"Each one of you in your own sphere, however obscure, can give Me nobly, heroically, love for love." *(M.T., no. 97).*

"Love Me more—oh, much more!—than human beings love one another." *(M.T., no. 134).*

17

LOVE
Why God Loves Us

"But always remember that if I love you it is because you are little, not because you are good." *(J.M., p.48)*.

"Do not forget that it is your nothingness and littleness that act as magnets to attract Me to you." *(J.M., p.80)*.

[To religious:] "I do not love you for what you are . . . but for what you are not, that is to say, your wretchedness and nothingness, for thus I have found a place for My greatness and bounty." *(J.M., p.208)*.

"They [souls] have not understood My Heart. For it is their very destitution and failings that incline My goodness towards them. And when, acknowledging their helplessness and weakness, they humble themselves and have recourse to Me trustfully, then indeed they give Me more glory than before their fault." *(J.M., p.422)*.

"Josefa, why do you love Me?" [Josefa:] "Lord, because Thou art so good." [Jesus:] "And I love you because you are so wretched and so lowly." *(J.M., p.436)*.

"I am not attracted by your merits but by My love for souls." *(J.M., p.260)*.

"Your misery attracts Me. What would you do without Me? Do not forget that the lowlier you become, the nearer I shall be to you. Let Me do as I please." *(J.M., p.46)*.

"I love you because you are so, so wretched. Do you not feel how much I love you? I love you because you cannot do without Me, and because I long to see you happy; I love you because I have given My life for you." *(M.T., no. 25)*.

"I love you because you have always loved Me. You did not know it was I whom you loved in cherishing your family and those whom I placed in your path; you did not know it was I whom you loved in them and whom you wished never to grieve." *(M.T., no. 37)*.

"It is not on account of your qualities that I love you, or on account of your virtues, if you had any. If you had any virtue, you would owe it to Me. Your own part would consist merely in having received My gift . . . It is not because of your defects or sins that I love you. It is because I have given you life, and because I continue to give it to you each day. And it is because I have redeemed you at the price of so much suffering. Because I am Love, all Love, I cannot cease communicating to My creatures the joy of loving! The joy of sharing My happiness!" *(M.T., no. 488)*.

18

LOVE
Its Value

"I do not look at the act itself, I look at the intention. The smallest act, if done out of love, acquires such merit that it gives Me immense consolation. . . . I want only love, I ask for nothing else." *(J.M., p.193)*.

"The obstinacy of a guilty soul wounds My Heart deeply, but the tender affection of one who loves Me not only heals the wound, but turns away the effects of My Father's Justice." *(J.M., p.368)*.

[Jesus told Josefa to say these words:] "I come from love and I go to love." [Then He added:] "Whether you go up or down, you are ever in My Heart, for it is an abyss of love." *(J.M., p.49)*.

"I want you to give Me souls. Only love in all you do is required. Suffer because you love, work because you love, and above all abandon yourself to love." *(J.M., p.54)*.

"Although you can do no more than desire to see Me loved, this is already much. It relieves My Heart. For this longing is love." *(J.M., p.114)*.

"I still have many souls who love Me and belong to Me. A single one of them can purchase pardon for a great many others who are cold and ungrateful." *(J.M., p.118)*.

"Understand this well, Josefa: when a soul loves Me, she can make up for many who offend Me, and this relieves My Heart." *(J.M., p.235)*.

"It is love that makes reparation, because that which offends God in sin is the absence of love." *(M.T., no. 109)*.

"As you need to feel yourselves loved so that you may blossom and open out to life, so do I need to feel Myself loved by you so that I may send you My gifts." *(M.T., no. 237)*.

"I desire to be loved; I crave the love of My creatures! When they will come to love Me, they will no longer offend Me. When two people really love each other, they never offend each other." *(C.B., p.98)*.

"I know that the fire of love is more sanctifying than that of Purgatory." *(St. Therese of the Child Jesus)*.

"Remain calm also in your act of love. For if you do not proceed with calmness but force your heart, the latter will become exhausted and will not be able to continue with its song! You must not think that it is less intense when it is more calm! Calmness insures its continuity, do you understand? Love is a fire in itself. Permit it to consume quietly My little victim! Love in peace. Let love consume you softly, not with fury and vehemence, for that would merely exhaust you and keep you from delighting Me with your song!" *(C.B., p.150-151)*.

"Tell all souls, Consolata, that I prefer an act of love and a Communion of love to any other gift which they may offer Me! Yes, an act of love is better than the discipline, for I thirst for love. Poor souls! They think that in order to reach Me it is necessary to live an austere, penitential life! . . . See how they misrepresent Me. They make Me out as one to be feared, whereas I am kindness itself! See how they forget the precept which I have given them, the very essence of the entire Law: 'Thou shalt love the Lord thy God with thy whole heart, with thy whole soul . . .'" *(C.B., p.75-76)*.

"Oh, if you could know the great value of one act of love!" *(C.B., p.142)*.

"Love without limit, My little daughter; love to folly, and you will know Me better." *(M.T., no. 107)*.

"You cannot live without being loved and without loving. When it is not God or some of your fellow creatures that you love, you love yourself. Love is as the breath of your soul. Love must be spoken of with respect because it comes from God. It must be received as a messenger from God, as His Spirit. It is an impulse which you receive, but which does not come from you, and which is divine in its source." *(M.T., no. 291).*

"Remember that, like yourself, your Sisters need to feel themselves loved; it is a necessity, because you are creatures in a state of evolution, and you *need* the love of others in order to develop." *(M.T., no. 414).*

"Love them [your Sisters] because they need it to become better, as you yourself need to be loved to become better. A person who feels herself loved becomes capable of every form of generosity." *(M.T., no. 525).*

"The soul that honors Me most is not the one who has suffered most—it is the one who has most perfectly transformed all her sufferings into love and joy—yes, all her sufferings, even the smallest annoyances and little disappointments. Her love glorifies Me already on earth." *(M.T., no. 633).*

"Today, as yesterday and tomorrow, I ask only and always for love from My poor creatures!" *(C.B., p.76).*

"Do you know what I desire from you? Continuous intimacy, without even an instants' distraction; always united with Me, even when you must converse with creatures." *(C.B., p.77).*

"My little daughter, all that you do to others is *really* done to Me." *(M.T., no. 414).*

"Yes, My Heart gives divine worth to these little offerings, for what I want is love! I am in search of love. I love souls and I look for a response of love. . . . I am Love and desire only love." *(J.M., p.196).*

19

MARY

[Mary:] "On Calvary, Jesus gave me all men for my sons; come then, for you are my child. . . . O how I love to think of Him as He bequeathed those souls to me." *(J.M., p.84)*.

[Mary:] "My choicest title to glory is that of being immaculate at the same time as being Mother of God. But my greatest joy is to add to this title that of Mother of mercy, and Mother of sinners." *(J.M., p.430)*.

[Jesus:] "Behold the Blessed Virgin at the foot of the Cross. She suffers, yes; but what dignity in her suffering! Can you see her? . . . In a sea of anguish, not one lament! She does not become despondent or discouraged; nothing of the kind! . . . She accepts and suffers; she offers it all up with calmness and strength, even to the *'Consummatum est.'* That is the way I wish you to be in the days of sorrow; the virginal purity of your love will help you to be so!" *(C.B., p.145-146)*.

"Think of My Mother, whom I have given to you to be your Mother also. Who has been charged with heavier responsibilities than she? Yet she was always calm and smiling because I filled her whole soul." *(M.T., no. 55)*.

"You will not understand till you get to Heaven what you owe to My Mother, and the gift that was made you when I gave her to you to be your Mother. How impenetrable is the love of God, who created for you the Virgin Mary, Mediatrix of all Graces!" *(M.T., no. 110)*.

"Look at My Mother: silent, self-effacing. What did she say? Only a few words of hers are known. She spoke in actions. What did she do? Her ordinary daily duty, without noise. She gave very great glory to God because she *was*. She was content to be what God wished her to be, and in the way He wished it. It is sufficient to be." *(M.T., no. 210)*.

"It is when a soul forgives and is silent that she most resembles My Mother." *(M.T., no. 259)*.

"You do well to feel compassion for My Mother. You will never feel too much when you think of the Way of the Cross. She shared all My sufferings; she drank the bitter chalice to the dregs; with Me she worked your Redemption. You must adore rather than seek to understand this mystery of her cooperation: It is one of the Father's mercies . . ." *(M.T., no. 469)*.

"Never appear alone before the Most Holy Trinity, but always with Me who prays within you, and with My Mother. We have adopted you, and you have given Me your humanity: I wish to live again in you . . ." *(M.T., no. 427)*.

[Mary:] "My child, the Church honors me today by contemplating my Immaculate Conception. Men admire in me the wonders wrought by God, and the beauty with which He clothed me even before Original Sin could stain my soul. He who is the Eternal God chose me for His Mother and overwhelmed my soul with graces greater than any bestowed on a creature. All the beauty you see in me is a reflection of the divine perfections, and the praises given me glorify Him who, being my Creator, willed to make me His Mother." *(J.M., p.430)*.

"See, in the Cribs they place Me not on My Mother's lap, but on the straw; because she did not keep Me for herself; she gave Me to the human race even before My birth." *(M.T., no. 188)*.

"I have made Myself so truly your Brother that I have willed that we should have the same Father—and that she who was the Mother of My Humanity should also be your Mother. Have I not treated you as an equal, as My friend . . .?" *(M.T., no. 279)*.

20

MERCY
The Forgiveness of God

"Never does My Heart refuse to forgive a soul that humbles itself, especially when it asks with confidence." *(J.M., p.91).*

"My Heart takes comfort in forgiving. I have no greater desire, no greater joy, than when I can pardon a soul. When a soul returns to Me after a fall, the comfort she gives Me is a gain for her, for I regard her with very great love." *(J.M., p.94).*

"I am consumed with desire to pardon. . . . Yes, to pardon these dear souls for whom I shed My Blood." *(J.M., p.136).*

"I will make known that the measure of My love and mercy for fallen souls is limitless. I want to forgive them. It rests Me to forgive." *(J.M., p.174).*

"My Heart is not so much wounded by sin, as torn with grief that they will not take refuge with Me after it." *(J.M., p.188).*

"All human miseries are known to My Heart, and My compassion for them is great." *(J.M., p.214).*

"Poor sinners, how blind they are! I want only to forgive them, and they seek only to offend Me. That is My great sorrow; that so many are lost and that they do not all come to Me to be forgiven." *(J.M., p.237).*

[Josefa asked if He remembered our faults after they were forgiven. Jesus replied:] "As soon as a soul throws itself at My feet and implores My forgiveness, Josefa, I forget all her sins." *(J.M., p.237).*

[If one is aroused from a state of tepidity:] "As soon as your soul is touched by grace, and before the struggle has even

begun, hasten to My Heart; beg of Me to let a drop of My
Blood fall on your soul. . . . Ah! Hasten to My Heart . . . and
be without fear for the past; all has been swallowed up in the
abyss of My mercy, and My love is preparing new graces for
you. The memory of your lapses will be an incentive to
humility and a source of merit, and you cannot give Me a
greater proof of affection than to count on My full pardon
and to believe that your sins will never be as great as My
mercy, which is infinite." *(J.M., p.289)*.

"I pursue sinners as justice pursues criminals. But justice
seeks them in order to punish, I, in order to forgive." *(J.M.,
p.237-238)*.

"The mercy of God is infinite and never refuses to forgive
sinners . . ." *(J.M., p.256)*.

"I want them all [souls] to have confidence in My mercy, to
expect all from My clemency, and never to doubt My
readiness to forgive. I am God, but a God of love! I am a
Father, but a Father full of compassion and never harsh. My
Heart is infinitely holy but also infinitely wise, and knowing
human frailty and infirmity, stoops to poor sinners with
infinite mercy.

"I love those who after a first fall come to Me for pardon. . . .
I love them still more when they beg pardon for their second
sin, and should this happen again, I do not say a million
times, but a million million times, I still love them and
pardon them, and I will wash in My Blood their last as fully
as their first sin.

"Never shall I weary of repentant sinners, nor cease from
hoping for their return, and the greater their distress, the
greater My welcome. Does not a father love a sick child with
special affection? Are not his care and solicitude greater? So
is the tenderness and compassion of My Heart more
abundant for sinners than for the just." *(J.M., p.353)*.

"However great is the number of your frailties, far greater
are the mercies of My Heart. . . . My love never changes."
(J.M., p.374).

"It takes so little to shake you . . . but have no fear; My mercy and love are infinitely greater, and your weakness will never surpass My strength." *(J.M., p.276).*

"Do not worry about your miseries; My Heart is the Throne of Mercy, and the most wretched are the best welcomed, as long as they come to lose themselves in the abyss of My love." *(J.M., p.120).*

"I make little account of all that [their miseries and weakness], provided souls come to Me with confidence and love. I Myself make up for all their frailty." *(J.M., p.133).*

"You cannot know how My heart exults in forgiving faults that are of pure frailty." *(J.M., p.156).*

"Oh! If souls only realized how I wait for them in mercy. I am the love of all loves, and it is My joy to forgive." *(J.M., p.196).*

"Consolata, you must never forget that I always am, and love to be, kind and merciful toward My creatures." *(C.B., p.42).*

[One time Consolata was lamenting her faults:] "Oh Jesus, I am always the same; I promise, and then . . ." And He replied: "I also am always the same and never change!" *(C.B., p.49).*

"Jesus is not a tyrant, and if He forgives an entire lifetime of crime in return for one act of love, then tell Me, how could it be that He would take notice one day of some useless thought on which you had dwelt involuntarily?" *(C.B., p.51).*

"Look, Consolata, the enemy will make every effort to shake your blind faith in Me, but you must never forget that I am, and love to be, exclusively kind and merciful. Understand My heart, Consolata; understand My love, and never permit the enemy to gain entrance into your soul, even for an instant, with a thought of diffidence; never! Believe Me, I am solely and always kind; I am solely and always like a parent to you! Imitate therefore the children who, at every little scratch of the finger, run at once to mother to have it

bandaged. You should always do the same, and remember
that I will always cancel out and repair your imperfections
and infidelities, just as the mother will always bandage the
child's finger, whether it is really hurt or only seems so in
imagination. And if the child were to really hurt his arm or
his head, how tenderly and affectionately would he be cared
for and bandaged by the mother! Well, I do the very same
with regard to your soul when you fall, even though I may do
it in silence. Do you understand, Consolata? Therefore,
never, never, never have even a shadow of doubt! Lack of
confidence wounds My Heart to the quick and makes Me
suffer!" *(C.B., p.53-54)*.

"No, My dear, I will not let you break your arm or your
head! But then you must also know that what I am now
saying to you, will one day be of use to other souls. That is
why I wish you to write it all down." *(C.B., p.54)*.

"It is My joy to pardon. If pride prevents you from being
sorry for your sins for your own sake, be sorry for them out
of love for Me, so that I may have the joy of forgiving . . ."
(M.T., no. 426).

"As soon as a soul opens herself, My Spirit takes possession
of her, quietly but victoriously. And what is there that I
cannot repair when I am allowed to do it? Then it is I who
have the pleasure of adorning your soul according to My
tastes and My good pleasure." *(M.T., no. 269)*.

"I will teach sinners that the mercy of My Heart is
inexhaustible." *(J.M., p.353)*.

"I never refuse grace even to those who are guilty of grave
sin; nor do I separate them from the good whom I love with
predilection. I keep them all in My Heart, that all may
receive the help required by their state of soul. . . ." *(J.M.,
p.234)*.

"At the least sign of repentance, My Heart is aflame with joy,
and I wait with *inexpressible* love for the sinner to turn
towards Me . . ." *(M.T., no. 157)*.

MISERY

"Your littleness is nothing to Me, and even your falls; My Blood wipes them all away. All you need do is to rely on My love and surrender yourself." *(J.M., p.82)*.

"Yes, say again that you love Me. It matters little to Me if you fall again.... I love your misery, Josefa!" *(J.M., 1st ed., p.208)*.

"If I have chosen you who are poor and miserable, it is that all may realize once more that I want neither greatness nor holiness ... but only love. I myself will do all the rest." *(J.M., p.202)*.

"When a soul comes to Me for strength, I do not leave her to herself; I hold her up, and if in her weakness she stumbles, I will raise her." *(J.M., p.240)*.

"Why fear? The more miseries I find in you, the more love you will find in Me." *(J.M., p.394)*.

"If you are an abyss of miseries, I am an abyss of mercy and goodness." *(J.M., p.92)*.

"That is true [that you are wretched and incapable], but do you know how little your wretchedness matters to Me? ... What I want is to be Master of your wretchedness." *(J.M., p.237)*.

"What does all the rest matter? ... Your sins? Why, I can wipe them out.... Your miseries? I consume them.... Your weakness? I will be its support.... Let us remain united." *(J.M., p.336)*.

"See how I refuse you nothing, and would you refuse Me anything?" [Josefa:] "I told Him that He knew my desires, but that my infirmity is greater than my will." *(J.M., 1st ed., p.177).*

"What does their [souls'] helplessness matter? Cannot I supply all their deficiencies? I will show how My Heart uses their very weakness to give life to many souls that have lost it." *(J.M., p.174).*

"It is because you are so little that you are able to creep so deeply into My Heart." *(J.M., p.203).*

"I want you to be nothing, that I may be All. The smaller a thing is, the more easily it can be handled. It is just because you are so paltry a thing that I can use you as I like." *(J.M., p.342).*

[Regarding the words of the Gospel, "Without Me you can do nothing":] "This is for you the most comforting saying in the Gospel, because it excuses all your weaknesses and throws you in complete abandonment upon the Heart of God. There, dissolved in a single act of love, you may ask what you will, and it will be granted you!" *(C.B., p.129-130).*

"Look, Consolata, your poverty is limited, but My love has no limits!" *(C.B., p.49).*

[Regarding involuntary faults:] "You see, Consolata, My Heart is won more readily through your wretchedness than through your virtues! Who came away from the Temple justified? The publican. For to Me the sight of a humble and contrite soul is irresistible . . . That is the way I am." *(C.B., p.52).*

"You must not grieve overmuch at your falls. Why, I could make a saint of you without more ado." *(J.M., p.52-53).*

"Do not let your falls, however many, trouble you. It is trouble and worry that keep a soul from God. Beg pardon, and I say again, tell your Mother [Superior] at once. . . ." *(J.M., 1st ed., p.126).*

"I will make it known that My work rests on nothingness and misery—such is the first link in the chain of love that I have prepared for souls from all eternity. I will use you to show that I love misery, littleness and absolute nothingness." *(J.M., p.174)*.

"Souls that see themselves overwhelmed with miseries attribute nothing good to themselves, and their very abjectness clothes them with a certain humility that they would not have if they saw themselves to be less imperfect." *(J.M., p.218)*.

"I will tell My chosen souls that My love for them goes further still; not only shall I make use of their daily life and of their least actions, but I will make use of their very wretchedness . . . their frailties . . . even of their falls, for the salvation of souls. Love transforms and divinizes everything, and mercy pardons all." *(J.M., p.216)*.

"With ruins, on ruins, I can build magnificently. It gives Me joy to use that which has humbled itself before Me, because My action is free." *(M.T., no. 278)*.

"I will reveal to souls the excess of My love and how far I will go in forgiveness, and how even their faults will be used by Me with blind indulgence . . . yes, write . . . with *blind indulgence.* I see the very depths of souls, I see how they would please, console and glorify Me, and the act of humility they are obliged to make when they see themselves so feeble is solace and glory to My Heart. What does their helplessness matter? Cannot I supply all their deficiencies? I will show how My Heart uses their very weakness to give life to many souls that have lost it." *(J.M., p.174)*.

[Mary:] "Do not regard your wretchedness, but look at the treasure that is yours, for if you are all His, He is all yours." *(J.M., p.172)*.

"Do not reflect on your helplessness; My Heart is powerful enough to sustain you. It is yours; take from It all you need. Be consumed in It . . . offer this Heart and this Blood to the Eternal Father." *(J.M., p.136)*.

"I require nothing of you beyond what is already yours. Give Me an empty heart and I will fill it . . . give Me a heart destitute of all adornment and I will make it beautiful. Give it to Me with all its miseries and I will consume them. What is hidden from you I will reveal, and all that you lack, I take on Myself to supply." *(J.M., p.346)*.

"Why these fears? Have I not told you that My one desire is to forgive? Do you think that I have chosen you because of your virtues? I know well that you have nothing but misery and weakness, but as I am a purifying fire, I will wrap you round in the flame of My Heart and destroy you. Ah! Josefa, how often I have told you that My one longing is for souls to bring Me their miseries! Come . . . and let Love consume you." *(J.M., p.345-346)*.

"You know that it is the property of fire to destroy and to enkindle. In the same way, My Heart's property is to pardon, love, and purify. Never think that I shall cease to love you because of your miseries. No, My Heart loves you and will never forsake you." *(J.M., p.344)*.

"Have no fear about your wretchedness and misery, your carelessness or even your faults. . . . I Myself will supply for all. My Heart is the Repairer par excellence. How, then, could it not be so for you?" *(J.M., p.376-377)*.

22

NATURAL GOODS AND THEIR USE

"When you take your food, think that you are giving Me that alleviation, and do the same whenever you take pleasure in anything whatsoever." *(J.M., p.100).*

[As Josefa had visitors, she asked Jesus not to mind if she did not speak directly to Him so often these days, but to take all spoken to them as also to Him, as she did it for love of Him. Jesus appeared and said:] "Have no misgivings on this head. I am as much consoled as if you were with Me. See Me in them, and live in peace." *(J.M., p.170).*

"My little daughter, see what a bad master Matter is: it turns against those who serve it and imprisons them within its own limitations. On the other hand, all the time, all the care that you give to the Spirit frees you from what is perishable." *(M.T., no. 85).*

"The greatest danger for you in the religious life is to seek consolation in the companionship of creatures and to prefer your illusions to My demands. Then you have no experience of My yoke—you take only part of it; so you cannot discover how easy that yoke is and how light is My burden . . ." *(M.T., no. 146).*

"Because My demands are more spiritual—known only to God!—than visible, and My rewards more spiritual than visible, hidden from the eyes of men, immediate satisfactions, visible joys are preferred to Me . . . I am banished from nations, banished everywhere." *(M.T., no. 342).*

"The love that you must have for creatures is not an end in itself; it is the consequence of your love for Me; I do not enter into rivalry with creatures, but I envelop and penetrate them, and you find them all again in My Heart." *(M.T., no. 414).*

"It is so: you are created for God; what creatures give you does not satisfy you. That which is human and natural in you most often irritates and wounds you." *(M.T., no. 575).*

"If you linger here and there to glean natural joys, you no longer need supernatural joys—it is you who are the cause of their rarity. You must choose." *(M.T., no. 624).*

"In the religious life you are happy inasmuch as you free yourselves from creatures in order to live alone with Me—yes, alone with Me, at My service." *(M.T., no. 225).*

"Yes, work is a joy and a great dignity for man; but what I desire is not merely your work, but *yourself.* You dishonor Me when you leave Me to think only of your work." *(M.T., no. 16).*

"Listen, you must not attach great importance to natural activity. *'Without Me you can do nothing.'* It is the spirit of the world that desires natures who are 'organizers,' 'efficient,' as they say when praising them. It is easy to make a stir, to work in a visible, outward manner; it is very difficult to renounce oneself and to let Me work. And yet that is the only fruitful activity, which lasts throughout eternity. Rest in Me. Depend on Me . . ." *(M.T., no. 71).*

"I await you in material work in which I have such need to be served with perfection—but I also await you in stillness and freedom of mind, in order to surrender Myself to your gaze." *(M.T., no. 231).*

23

OBEDIENCE AND SUPERIORS

"Do you not know where to find Me, Josefa? . . . One of the visible proofs of My love is that I have given you two Mothers [Superiors] to love and help you. Seek Me in them. There you will always find Me." *(J.M., 1st ed., p.178).*

"I have drawn you to My Heart that obedience may be your very breath . . . know this, that if I should ask one thing of you and your Superiors another, I prefer you to obey them rather than Me." *(J.M., p.418).*

"Seek Me in your Superiors. Listen to their words as if they fell from My lips; I am in them for your guidance." *(J.M., p.418).*

"When I see those who love Me obey with difficulty, it humiliates Me; when prayer, when virtue costs them something, it humiliates Me: I who have said that My yoke is easy and My burden light! Serve Me with a heart that sings!" *(M.T., no. 219).*

"Obedience is charity in action. It covers all your sins." *(M.T., no. 299).*

"How would you have My blessing if you do not receive that of your Superior?" *(M.T., no. 574).*

"Your Superior's wish is My wish." *(M.T., no. 236).*

"If you saw My disappointment in the lives of religious who founder in selfishness, you would die." *(M.T., no. 523).*

"In the same way as you try to please your Spouse, strive to please your Superiors; anticipate their desires; do what they like, that they may feel themselves loved by you, loved in a special way." *(M.T., no. 10).*

"It is very pleasing to Me that you submit in everything to your Superior's authority, because authority comes from God; I desire not only that you should submit to it, but that you should love your Superior . . . that you should love My likeness in her, yes, My own likeness that needs to feel itself loved so that it may radiate through her." *(M.T., no. 261).*

"The obedient soul, the soul that is in the state of obedience, has her eyes open to My Presence; without leaving it, she finds signs of it everywhere, and My messages also, because she yields immediately to what I say to her. When she has placed herself in this state of abandonment, of silence and calm, it is as if she were unable to detach herself from Me; she embraces every contradiction, every suffering, as a gift she has to offer Me, and nothing disturbs her serenity." *(M.T., no. 361).*

"Obedience is a state of the soul, a permanent state which makes the soul cling perseveringly to the will of God, and immediately to the manifold opportunities which she is given to submit her own will to that of others. Obedience, My little daughter, is something very deep and very powerful, yes, even irresistible, with the Heart of God." *(M.T., no. 354).*

"When a soul is willing to receive enlightenment from her Superiors, to obey them through love and the spirit of faith, she is ready to receive the greatest graces; this dependence removes obstacles between her and Me. But it must be real dependence, interior and voluntary, otherwise it is in vain." *(M.T., no. 401).*

"When you obey your Superiors, their imperfections, whatever they may be, take nothing away from the perfection of your obedience: it is always I whom you obey. That is enough." *(M.T., no. 440).*

"Once a soul has knowledge of the state of obedience, she can no longer bear to live outside that state because it unites you to Me." *(M.T., no. 436).*

"My little daughter, if it happens that you have a Superior who is rather severe, rather exacting where nature is concerned, rejoice! You must even thank Me for it. Extreme vigilance is required in the cloister to resist the natural inclinations of selfishness, and you need to be helped." *(M.T., no. 526).*

"To understand what I ask of you, you must submit your thoughts and desires to those whom I give you to enlighten your soul. I, too, only did the Father's will." *(M.T., no. 555).*

"Ah! Hasten to My Heart . . . you know that in your Superiors, whoever they may be . . . I am there concealed under the veil of faith. . . . Lift the veil and tell Me all about your sufferings, miseries and falls with complete confidence . . . receive My words with respect and be without fear for the past; all has been swallowed up in the abyss of My mercy, and My love is preparing new graces for you. . . ." *(J.M., 1st ed., p.312).*

"If you have been obedient to your Rule in everything, to your Superior and to your Father, and to what I have said to you . . . that is enough. I will do the rest." *(M.T., no. 276).*

"Each time you obey, you offer Me through visible actions the invisible love with which I fill your heart." *(M.T., no. 150).*

POVERTY

"When you have all that is necessary, you deprive Me of the joy of taking care of you." *(M.T., no. 1).*

"I wish to see you before Me, poor and stripped, without possessions, so that I may daily enrich you with new gifts . . ." *(M.T., no. 117).*

"Your joy is to strip yourselves and to be dependent on Me alone. My joy is to be able to prove to you the prodigality of My love." *(M.T., no. 126).*

"My little daughter, beware of avarice. It unconsciously introduces itself into a soul. It shuts the soul out from My Kingdom. Avarice is the cause of lying—of all crimes, of all denials, of all treason. The attachment to passing goods which one desires to possess and to hold, hates My Spirit and wishes to destroy It. Avarice is the work of death." *(M.T., no. 273).*

" 'My Kingdom is not of this world'—that is why I do not seek to make My Royalty resplendent in this world of Matter. I dominate Matter and merely lend Myself to it. That is why I seek, by preference, an appearance of poverty, where Matter is very little honored; thus I am within reach of everyone; thus you will be able to understand that it is by freeing yourselves from Matter that you will discover the world of the Spirit. Give, give, make yourself poor, so that there may be in you and around you only one beauty, your Jesus!" *(M.T., no. 189).*

"Become entirely *poor* in words, in actions, in objects, in desires, apart from your union with Me and My will—It is I who will live in you. Let Me do it, My beloved." *(M.T., no. 12).*

PRAYER

"Yes, pray . . . pray . . . do not grow tired nor fear to be importunate, for prayer is the key that opens every door." *(J.M., p.325).*

"Think of Me all the time. Souls glorify Me so much when they remember Me." *(J.M., p.210).*

"You remain near Me, but your mind is saturated with mere nothings! It is as if you fell asleep at My Feet while My Heart was calling you." *(M.T., no. 245).*

"By means of unceasing prayer, prepare the triumph of My Heart and of My love throughout the earth!" *(C.B., preface).*

"Tell Me, what more beautiful prayer do you want to offer Me? 'Jesus, Mary, I love You! Save souls!' Love and souls! What more beautiful prayer could you desire?" *(C.B., p.163).*

"You think you do not know how to pray? . . . What prayer is more beautiful and more acceptable to Me than the act of love? Do you know what Jesus is doing in the tabernacle? He is loving the Father and He is loving souls. That is all. No sound of words, nothing. Only silence and love. So, do the same! No, my dear, do not add any prayers; no, no, no! Gaze upon the tabernacle, and love in that way!" *(C.B., p.164).*

"I withdrew into the Garden of Gethsemane, that is to say into solitude. God is to be sought within, away from distraction and noise. To find Him the soul must enforce silence on all the disturbances by which nature often fights against grace; on interior arguments prompted by self-love or sensuality. These constantly tend to stifle the inspirations of grace and keep her from finding God within." *(J.M., p. 259).*

"I prefer one of your acts of love to all your prayers! 'Jesus,

Mary, I love You! Save souls!' This comprises all: the souls
in Purgatory and those in the Church Militant, the innocent
and the sinful souls, the dying, the godless, etc." *(C.B.,
p.164)*.

"To speak or to listen to Me are two different kinds of
prayer." [Consolata:] "My Lord Jesus, which do You
prefer?" [Jesus:] "That which listens to Me." *(M.T., no. 130)*.

[In answer to Josefa's question—Why do prayers made for
some sinners seem to be of no avail?] "When a soul prays for
a sinner with an intense desire for his conversion, his prayer
generally obtains the sinner's conversion, though sometimes
only at the last moment, and the offence given to My Heart
is repaired. But in any case, prayer is never lost, for on the
one hand, it consoles Me for the pain sin has occasioned, and
on the other, its efficacy and power are applied, if not to that
sinner, then to others better disposed to profit by it." *(J.M.,
p.234)*.

"I was telling you yesterday how little such souls really
know Me. . . . It is the same when they pray, either for
themselves or for others; if they waver and doubt, they do
not glorify My Heart, but they do glorify It if they are sure
that I shall give them what they ask, knowing that I refuse
them nothing that is good for their souls." *(J.M., p.422)*.

"Do you understand, My little daughter, that in the majority
of souls I find tumult? Conflicting desires in opposition to
the prayers which the lips pronounce. You must *desire* what
you ask of Me in words; you must also pray by your desires."
(M.T., no. 441).

PRESENCE OF GOD

"I am always with you even when you do not see Me." *(J.M., p.262).*

"I am so immersed in you that I agree to become *you* in order to win you entirely. But I am also outside you." *(M.T., no. 243).*

"You would not be able to bear the sight of Me; that is why I hide Myself in countenances within reach of you: in the faces that surround you, the faces of duty, of pain, and of pleasure—I am always hidden in the Cross." *(M.T., no. 562).*

"It is easy to live in My intimacy, by conversing with Me. I desire that of each soul." *(M.T., no. 617).*

"When you are in pain, do you not feel that I am there, that it is I who sustain, who carry you . . .? Am I not enough for you? What do you desire?" *(M.T., no. 235).*

"I am your life. Do you understand that? I am as inseparable from you as your breathing, as the breath within your soul. I am so near to you." *(M.T., no. 29).*

"I am living in the Blessed Sacrament, in the Real Presence . . . I, the Real Presence, am also living in each soul that is in the state of grace. Why do you not, in spirit, adore My Presence in your neighbor?" *(M.T., no. 143).*

"Ah, if you understood! How happy each soul could be in My intimacy! The pettinesses that *blind* you would, of themselves, disappear in this ever-growing quest for Love— and I am Love, I who answer as soon as I am called . . . I give Myself to all souls; but I have secrets to give each one that are for her alone, with her mission which is hers alone . . ." *(M.T. no. 169).*

PROVIDENCE

"Fear nothing. My work is wrought in the dark, but when it sees the light, all will wonder at its every detail." *(J.M., p.390).*

[St. Madeleine-Sophie Barat:] "Jesus Himself is arranging everything, and difficult as it may appear to creatures, He ordains each event in the way best for His plan." *(J.M., p.433).*

"Ah, if you knew how the Holy Trinity watches over you! You are lost, carried in its solicitude as a child in the womb of its mother—and like that child you are unaware of your happiness. Open your understanding to the ceaseless messages which reveal it to you." *(M.T., no. 240).*

"Thus do I change the circumstances in your lives to make them work together for the greater good of your soul—that is a mere game for divine power! And that same power can do nothing in your soul, without your acquiescence." *(M.T., no. 628).*

"It seems to you that you see nothing and that you are about to fall into the precipice. But need you see, if you are guided?" *(J.M., p.68).*

"As My Providence provides your daily bread that your body may live, so it is My very tender Providence that provides you with what comes to you daily in the way of fresh sacrifices, occasions for practicing the virtues you have asked of Me, so that you may be living souls, growing daily in My knowledge and My love. Think of this when suffering comes." *(M.T., no. 120).*

"Yes, My power is infinite: beyond all that your thoughts can imagine. You have a presentiment of it when you see that the means which appear to be employed for one specific end, I use at the same time for a multitude of other causes ... Remember this: everything is a means in My Hands; I make all work together to fulfill My will. With My grace, for you too, everything becomes a means—it is the way in which you use them that glorifies Me and reveals your generosity." (M.T., no. 132).

"Yes, I attend to these details of your life—you are amazed at it! As a mother interests herself in all that concerns her newborn infant, I interest Myself in all that affects you. I do not lower Myself by doing so because I am not a degree of greatness, I am Love, and Love remains great when manifesting itself among little things as well as among great things." (M.T., no. 168).

"It was a great glory for Simon the Cyrenean [to carry My Cross]. It is also for your glory when I honor you with sufferings. Accept them all as coming from Me. And remember that all I say to you, as all I send you—it is always because I love you and wish you to be altogether Mine ..." (M.T., no. 444).

"Do you think that anything happens without My permission? I dispose all things for the good of each and every soul. Though this hour seems dark to you, My power dominates it and My work will gain by it. I am your All, Josefa, so do not be afraid, for you are not alone. I have not brought you here for your ruin, but from love, and because it is fitting that all this should happen." (J.M., p.331).

"As you are very small, you must let yourself be controlled and guided by My fatherly hand which is powerful and infinitely strong. ... I will mold you as is best for My glory and for souls. ... Do not fear, for I am looking after you with jealous care, such care as the tenderest of mothers takes of her little child." (J.M., p.180).

28

REPARATION

"The obstinacy of a guilty soul wounds My Heart deeply, but the tender affection of one who loves Me not only heals the wound, but turns away the effects of My Father's Justice." *(J.M., p.368).*

"One single act of love in the loneliness in which I leave you repairs for many of the acts of ingratitude of which I am the object." *(J.M., p.53).*

"One faithful soul can repair and obtain mercy for many ungrateful ones." *(J.M., p.73).*

"My justice will be restrained as long as I find victims who will make reparation." *(J.M., p.190).*

"I know your wretchedness, Josefa, and I take on Myself to make reparation for it; you on your part, make reparation for souls." *(J.M., p.394).*

"Alas! The world offends Me, but it will be saved by the reparation of My chosen souls." *(J.M., p.410).*

"Love is reparation and reparation is love." *(J.M., p.410).*

"It is the obedience and love with which you contrive to offer Me your penance that moves Me." *(M.T., no. 42).*

"It is love that makes reparation, because that which offends God in sin is the absence of love." *(M.T., no. 109).*

"I ask . . . of My consecrated souls: *Reparation,* that is a life of union with Him who makes Divine Reparation: to work for Him, with Him, in Him, in a spirit of reparation, in close union with His feelings and desires." *(J.M., p.427).*

"You know that sin is an infinite offence and needs infinite reparation . . . that is why I ask you to offer up your sufferings and labors in union with the infinite merits of My Heart. You know that My Heart is yours. Take It, therefore, and repair by It." *(J.M., p.405).*

"Believe Me, My little daughter, each one of you, if she wishes to, can, in spite of the troubles of the cloister, console Me and make reparation for a great number of crimes." *(M.T., no. 264).*

"Do you know that there is . . . more happiness in making reparation than in doing additional good works? The soul that makes reparation gives Me two joys: she re-establishes order—and above all: she erases from My Heart the pain caused by the unfaithful soul, because by making reparation she arouses repentance—and nothing consoles Me so much as a repentant soul. She becomes My beloved . . ." *(M.T., no. 483).*

"It is love that makes reparation—it is love that leads to the folly of the Cross." *(M.T., no. 445).*

"I have need of acts of generosity that make reparation for the infidelities of those who are Mine. I have need of sacrifices, of hidden charity, that make reparation for destructive selfishness. I have need of acts of courage, of humble and true obedience that make reparation for falsehood, rebellion, the errors of pride . . ." *(M.T., no. 518).*

"The perfect fidelity of one single soul makes reparation for many." *(M.T., no. 524).*

"The soul that regrets her sin and makes reparation for it gives Me a greater proof of love than a soul that has avoided sin. She who has avoided it gives Me in an instant a passing proof of the solidity of her love; she who regrets and makes reparation offers Me repeated proofs of it. She becomes so dear to Me that I unite her to Myself. The other avoided sin because she was already united to Me . . ." *(M.T., no. 560).*

"The more I forgive you, the more you desire to do penance and make reparation. This desire must not be extinguished but enkindled in souls. It is the grace which flows immediately from My pardon." *(M.T., no. 186).*

"The sins committed are so many and so grave that the wrath of My Father would overflow were it not for the reparation and love of My consecrated brides. . . . How many souls are lost!" *(J.M., p. 72).*

"At the least sign of repentance, My Heart is aflame with joy, and I wait with *inexpressible* love for the sinner to turn towards Me . . . For terrible is the condition of an impenitent heart, I cannot penetrate it. It is not I who condemn it, it is he who willfully repels Me. Pray for the wicked, suffer and expiate for them. Ah, yes, make smooth the ways of the Lord!" *(M.T., no. 157).*

"My Heart is yours; take It and repair with It." *(J.M., p.181).*

29

SPIRITUAL LIFE
What Pleases God

"You cannot think, Josefa, how much glory your faith, your trust and your submission have given Me." *(J.M., p.397)*.

"You cannot give Me a greater proof of affection than to count on My full pardon and to believe that your sins will never be as great as My mercy, which is infinite." *(J.M., p.289)*.

"Do you know how to comfort Me? Love Me and suffer for souls and never refuse Me anything." *(J.M., p.157)*.

"I take pleasure in the expectant love of My friends. There are so many who never think of Me." *(J.M., p.187)*.

"I do not ask much from them [men], but I do ask their love." *(J.M., p.207)*.

"Think of Me all the time. Souls glorify Me so much when they remember Me." *(J.M., p.210)*.

"The soul who constantly unites her life with Mine glorifies Me and does a great work for souls." *(J.M., p.213)*.

"If I have chosen you who are poor and miserable, it is that all may realize once more that I want neither greatness nor holiness . . . but only love. I Myself will do all the rest." *(J.M., p.202)*.

[Mary:] "What pleases my Son most is love and humility . . ." *(J.M., p.269)*.

"That soul is dearest to Me who loves Me the most!" *(C.B., p.100)*.

[Josefa:] "He showed me clearly that what pleases Him most is to do little acts out of obedience." *(J.M., p.24).*

"One of your Communions recompenses Me for all I had to suffer in order to search you out, to find you and to possess you.... Your heart is Mine exclusively, and what else do I desire from My poor creatures, but the heart?" *(C.B., p.67).*

"If you only knew what joy it gives Me to sanctify a soul! Everybody ought to become holy in order to procure Me this pleasure! Would you like to have a faint idea of it? Then think of the joy which a mother feels when she sees her son return radiant with his well-earned diploma; the happiness of that mother is indescribable! Well, My felicity in seeing a soul attain sanctity vastly exceeds that faint comparison!" *(C.B., p.72).*

"A great number of souls consecrate themselves to My service—very few live *My life*—most of them live *their* life while working for Me. It is not thus that I glorified My Father—it is not thus that you glorify Me. Think of the sacrifices that human love demands: a wife makes the tastes of her husband her own, she gives way to his habits, adopts his ways, even his thoughts ... And their children bear the features of one and of the other. Should divine love remain below that standard?" *(M.T., no. 549).*

30

SPIRITUAL LIFE
Our Cooperation with Our Lord

"He showed me clearly that what pleases Him most is to do little acts out of obedience." *(J.M., p.24).*

"A little act of generosity, of patience, of poverty ... may become a treasure that will win a great number of souls to My Heart." *(J.M., p.175).*

"If the soul can keep calm, then she will remain master of herself; but if she is perturbed, then it is easy for her to fall." *(C.B., p.50).*

"It is interior effort that matters; it *is* for eternity; the visible result matters little, it is the interior effort which will produce fruit at harvest time." *(M.T., no. 249).*

"Do you think I could not grant you this continuity of love? It pleases Me to see you struggle, fall, and rise again, in short, making an effort. I like to see what you can do. And do you know what delights Me most? It is when you rise above everything unperturbed and continue your act of love!" *(C.B., p.125).*

"I do not ask you to free yourself, for I know it is not always in your power, but what I do ask of you is to keep up the struggle against your passions." *(J.M., p.263).*

"I do not tell you what you should know—I only tell you a tiny part; you must find out and understand for yourself; that is life. Oh, if you knew how much I need your cooperation." *(M.T., no. 211).*

"You ask Me for graces because you think of My omnipotence—why do you forget that My action depends on yours? It is with each soul as I said to St. Catherine of Siena:

'Your measure will be My measure.' When you ask for a grace, make yourselves able to bear the consequences, all the consequences, then with what joy I can immediately give it to you!" *(M.T., no. 215).*

"You must begin by being faithful in little things. My little daughter, console Me by being more faithful." *(M.T., no. 662).*

"When you show yourself [to your confessor] just as you are, with all your mediocrity, it is as if you had given Me a beautiful present—because then your Father will be able to find the remedy necessary for you. Then you have made a good confession." *(M.T., no. 214).*

"I wish each soul to understand that she has her special place in My Heart which awaits her; that her love is necessary to Me, and her cooperation necessary—that I need to see her happy and perfect—because I have loved her even to dying on the Cross for her—yes, each soul." *(M.T., no. 247).*

"I wish every soul to know that she has a greater motive for living than herself, one outside herself: to take part in the establishment of My Kingdom—and that her taking her part is necessary to Me in order that My creation may achieve the fullness of its destiny." *(M.T., no. 247).*

"Remember this: The value of your existence is not in what you have done, or said, or suffered: it is in the part of your being that you have given to your Saviour, in what you have allowed Me to do with you. Give Me your heart—and your heart is your whole life!" *(M.T., no. 349).*

"As My Providence provides your daily bread that your body may live, so it is My very tender Providence that provides you with what comes to you daily in the way of fresh sacrifices, occasions for practicing the virtues you have asked of Me, so that you may be living souls, growing daily in My knowledge and My love. Think of this when suffering comes." *(M.T., no. 120).*

"You, My Poor Clares, work through interior acts. God alone

sees them. That is the truest action; that which produces exterior action; it is that which *is,* and which lasts throughout eternity." *(M.T., no. 251).*

"I wish *each soul* to understand that My omnipotent Love transforms that which you give Me, working wonders with it for Eternity." *(M.T., no. 184).*

"The purpose of your life does not lie in the personal merit due to your generosity; your merit will lie in using all your generosity to allow Me to live in you. Do you understand?" *(M.T., no. 328).*

"Your life is very great. My little daughter, the least act of obedience, because it is done in union with Me, the least fidelity to your Holy Rule, has its repercussion on the entire Church. Would you believe it? In the same way your failings, the smallest of your acts of cowardice, has its repercussion on the entire world—by its consequences; would you believe it?" *(M.T., no. 643).*

~31~

SPIRITUAL LIFE
Hindrances and Evils

"If you saw My disappointment in the lives of religious who founder in selfishness, you would die." *(M.T., no. 523).*

"What is it that keeps you from loving Me, Consolata? It is useless thoughts and being interested in others!" *(C.B., p.90).*

"You see, Consolata, in Heaven every choir of angels attends to the fulfillment of its own office without envying or desiring the office of another. Thus, in a community, each one must attend to her own mission without envying or longing for something which pertains to another soul. In your community, in choir, and everywhere, you must be My little Seraph, and therefore you must attend solely to loving without envying or desiring the mission of your other Sisters!" *(C.B., p.91).*

"You must, under obedience, pay no attention to what your Sisters give Me! I and you, that suffices!" *(C.B., p.91).*

"My enemies are: lying, especially that lack of sincerity which paralyzes so many souls because they will not acknowledge to themselves their most hidden intentions; carelessness and ignorance due to laziness; agitation, disorder; noise: noise of words, noise of selfish desires, the noise that men invent to distract themselves and to forget Me." *(M.T., no. 92).*

"Many souls exhaust themselves in efforts, in acts of generosity, which leave their soul bruised and impoverished, because they strain at an ideal of virtue, of sanctity, that I do not ask of them. They will be rewarded for their pure intention and their generosity, but their efforts do not produce the fruit that they would produce if they were united to My will." *(M.T., no. 555).*

"All souls could rapidly attain to the plenitude of their sanctity if they allowed Me to act, without resisting. Oh, the unacknowledged reserves of selfishness which paralyze the omnipotence of the Holy Spirit within you!" *(M.T., no. 608).*

"The danger of the cloister lies in seeking in creatures, apart from Me, a distraction from your life of privation: I who am waiting for you! I, who am better than consolation—the Source of joy." *(M.T., no. 32).*

"When the devil wishes to spoil a religious community, he employs two great means: illusions and misunderstandings. Illusions introduce falsehood. Misunderstandings are the little accomplices that contrive between themselves finally to expel Me. I keep you from illusions if you submit your desires and thoughts to those whom I give you to enlighten your soul. Simplicity and sincerity are enough to destroy the worst misunderstandings." *(M.T., no. 569).*

"Sadness and melancholy find no place in the heart that loves Me; I fill it with My Cross and with joy." *(M.T., no. 258).*

"You must have compassion for souls who are nearing their eternity. They must be helped not to have a single bitter feeling, no suspicion of rancor, so that the love of creatures, human love, may open their heart to divine love and to its demands for sincerity." *(M.T., no. 614).*

32

SUFFERING

[Josefa:] "It is blindness to avoid pain even in very small things, for not only is it of great worth to ourselves, but it serves to guard many from the torments of Hell." *(J.M., p.145).*

"Suffering is necessary for all, but how much more for My chosen souls! . . . It purifies them, and I am thus able to make use of them to snatch many from Hell fire." *(J.M., p.230).*

[St. John the Evangelist:] "Suffering is the life of the soul, and the soul that has understood its value lives the true life." *(J.M., p.212).*

"Suffering, My little daughter, is the privilege of your life on earth. Do you not feel that I am there when you suffer? Oh, if you understood!" *(M.T., no. 557).*

"When suffering is accepted with love, it is no longer suffering, but is changed into joy." *(C.B., p.108).*

"Yes, Consolata, the hearts of the Littlest Ones are destined to die of love for Me and to consume themselves exclusively for Me. The world cannot call Me cruel, for ever so many die of vice, victims of the world! Is it not right, Consolata, that the creature should consume herself for her Creator?" *(C.B., p.192).*

"When I wish to attract a soul nearer to Me, I ask sacrifices of her: that is the mark of My predilection." *(M.T., no. 558).*

"I am always more sensitive, more active where there is suffering, because there I am welcomed, I am listened to . . ." *(M.T., no. 64).*

"I loved suffering, I the Man of Sorrows; I chose it because it makes reparation for sins when it is offered with love.... when suffering is joined to love, the proofs of love given through suffering are a true reparation offered to God. It is giving God something that He does not have in His Heaven. Therefore I chose suffering so that all My creatures, even the most miserable, like yourself, might have something precious to offer to God." *(M.T., no. 109)*.

"No, there is not a single superfluous suffering in your life. Your heart must be rent that My grace may penetrate it; otherwise you remain as a closed garden within your own feelings, your own thoughts, your horizon. Your horizon must be rent, so that you may catch a glimpse of the destiny to which you are called. Your destiny is so great that according to nature, you could not of yourselves imagine it. Your heart must be rent that My grace may penetrate and transform it." *(M.T., no. 164)*.

"I said I would draw all men to Me when I was lifted up from the earth. My little daughter, remember that and understand it. It was not in My hidden life or during My ministry that I drew all men to Me; it was after I had been lifted onto the Cross. It was a supreme and apparent destruction—yet a triumph of Love, of the Spirit of God. Do not be surprised if I invite those who are Mine to let themselves be destroyed by love." *(M.T., no. 376)*.

"Be persuaded that if your self-denial and suffering bear fruit but late or bear no fruit at all, they have not been in vain or useless. Some day you will bear abundant sheaves and reap a great reward." *(J.M., p.299)*.

"There is so much suffering in the world, suffering that crushes souls instead of uplifting them. The sacrifices I ask of you are not much—but I know what they cost you, that is why I ask ... Do you not want to be My little provider, of whom I can ask *everything?* Let yourself be stripped. Do you not wish to bear some resemblance to your Spouse?" *(M.T., no. 454)*.

33

TRIALS AND TEMPTATIONS

"When I leave you so cold, I am using your warmth to give heat to other souls. When I leave you a prey to anguish, your suffering wards off divine justice when it is about to strike sinners." *(J.M., p.51)*.

"See what your loving heart does to Mine, for though you feel cold and imagine you no longer love Me, it holds back My justice from punishing sinners." *(J.M., p.53)*.

"Do not think that I love you more, now that I console you, than when I ask you to suffer." *(J.M., p.132)*.

[Mary:] "It is good for you to love without knowing or feeling it." *(J.M., p.274)*.

"Josefa, do you not know that I and the Cross are inseparable? If you meet Me, you meet the Cross, and when you find the Cross, it is I whom you have found." *(J.M., p.328)*.

"Fear nothing. My work is wrought in the dark, but when it sees the light, all will wonder at its every detail." *(J.M., p.390)*.

[Josefa:] "O my God ... all that makes up this temptation— I offer it all to Thee ..." *(J.M., p.30)*.

"So, when an occasion of conquering human respect and accepting bravely either humiliation or suffering (even if it could easily be avoided) presents itself, a soul should answer: 'My Kingdom is not of this world' ..." *(J.M., p.277)*.

"Everything that distracts you from pious practices such as Holy Mass, Communion, the Divine Office, meditation, is not good, and proceeds not from Me." *(C.B., p.162)*.

"Do you desire the useless thoughts? No. Then everything is to your merit. When one desires only to love, then everything that obstructs that love becomes meritorious. Do you understand?" *(C.B., p.83).*

"I do not ask you to free yourself, for I know it is not always in your power, but what I do ask of you is to keep up the struggle against your passions." *(J.M., p.263).*

"When a trial befalls you, seek the cause *within yourselves:* what wrong have you done? What good are you neglecting to do? Be *conscious* of your responsibilities and the way in which you fulfill them. You must first understand, and then make amends. Then you will see that when the trial is no longer necessary, it will cease." *(M.T., no. 79).*

"Believe Me, it is with trials that I send My greatest graces. My love is watchful. A community that is not tried runs the risk of foundering in indifference." *(M.T., no. 133).*

"One opportunity of forgiving, of overcoming evil by good, is a great present on My part." *(M.T., no. 200).*

"I seek for rest in tender and protecting souls—who remain calm in the midst of all sufferings in order that My love may express itself, and unfold its immense wings ... You ask Me for love; accept suffering for Me and for souls: then you will love; love will possess you." *(M.T., no. 224).*

"The souls who surrender themselves to love never regret it. It is true that I break down the boundaries of their hearts, for the narrow horizon of their knowledge must be rent that they may catch a glimpse of the splendors of My Kingdom, the boundless world of the Spirit." *(M.T., no. 292).*

"It is not when everything is going well that you love Me. It is when everything is going wrong, and in spite of it your soul remains united to Me, peaceful, occupied only in diffusing a good spirit." *(M.T., no. 545).*

"Trials should produce a definite result in your souls; if you see that the trial ceases, lay hold of the virtue that it came to teach you, and practice it. Thus if you do your share of penance in your life, I shall not have to send you the sicknesses which take the place of neglected mortifications. In the same way, the more simple you are, the more you will avoid great temptations, which are used to destroy in you that which is an obstacle between you and Me." *(M.T., no. 328).*

"A little effort and pain, then such a great reward—and already here below the reward of seeing love, generosity, and the Faith spread irresistibly, like a spot of oil." *(M.T., no. 235).*

"See, My little daughter, I really have to send trials to those whom I love in order to wrench them out of the network of habits or of errors wherein you run the risk of burying yourself. 'The disciples are not above the Master': it is by the Cross that I saved the world." *(M.T., no. 429).*

"Just as storms are necessary in nature, so are they necessary in every living soul. Do not lose your serenity on account of those who are being tried. Pray for them: offer the sufferings of My Passion and some acts of self-denial, some self-imposed sufferings for them." *(M.T., no. 43).*

ZEAL FOR SOULS

[What to do in order to convert a sinner:] "You must put My Heart between the sinner and My Father, Josefa. My Heart will appease His wrath and incline divine compassion toward that soul." *(J.M., p.155)*.

[How to save many souls:] "Unite all you do to My actions, whether you work or whether you rest. Unite your breathing to the beating of My Heart. How many souls you would be able to save that way." *(J.M., p.83)*.

"I love souls madly, they must not be lost . . . Oh help Me in this undertaking of love." *(J.M., 1st ed., p.219)*.

"Each soul is a matchless treasure to Me." *(M.T., p.152)*.

"Nothing, indeed, is wanting to My heavenly beatitude, which is infinite, but I yearn for souls. . . . I thirst for them, and want to save them." *(J.M., p.377)*.

"Do not lose time! Every act of love means a soul!" *(C.B., p.128)*.

"Consolata, I am in need of victim-souls! The world is going to its ruin, but I wish to save it." *(C.B., p.33)*.

"Consolata, the devil one day swore he would ruin you, and I vowed I would save you . . . Satan also swore he would ruin the world, and I vowed I would save it; and I will save it through the triumph of My mercy and My love. Yes, I will save the world through My merciful love! Write this down." *(C.B., p.33)*.

"These horrors of the war are a small thing compared with the loss of souls. One must thank God if, by them, souls accept their salvation." *(M.T., no. 159)*.

"Remember that those who are vowed to My service receive encouragement in the measure that they love souls. If you have a great love for souls, you will discover many consolations which will escape you if you have but little love for souls. This is the secret of barren and radiant lives. For the aim of the religious life is 'God in souls.'" *(M.T., no. 187)*.

"Oh, how I thirst for souls—how I long for them to surrender themselves to Me so that I may transform them, for them to surrender their humanity to Me so that I may work in the world! Why do you not hear My call? Have I not exhausted every means to beg for your attention and your gratitude?" *(M.T., no. 231)*.

"It is impossible for you to know the value and the virtue of others, but you will never have too great a respect for souls, because I have redeemed them all at the price of My Blood." *(M.T., no. 582)*.

"Do you understand that you have worked for the whole world when through generosity you triumph over the little miseries that spread a bad spirit among you: you have made Me triumph over My enemies: My kingdom descends among you." *(M.T., no. 602)*.

"Already your littleness and sufferings have saved many souls . . ." *(J.M., p.207)*.

[Josefa:] " 'I saw souls fall into Hell in dense groups, and at times it was impossible to calculate their number." [Jesus:] "You have seen the fallen, Josefa, but you have not yet seen those who are saved and go up into Heaven!" [Josefa:] "Then I saw an innumerable crowd of souls, rank upon rank, and they entered into an illimitable space which was filled with resplendent light, and were lost in its immensity." *(J.M., p.204)*.

"I look only for love, docile love that allows itself to be led by the Lover . . . disinterested love, that seeks neither for pleasure nor for self-interest, but thinks only of the Beloved. Zealous love, burning, fiery and vehement love, that overcomes all the obstacles raised by egoism: that is true

94

love, love that snatches souls from the bottomless pit into which they cast themselves headlong." *(J.M., p.233-234).*

"My little daughter, here is an explanation which will astonish you; remember it, because it is the truth: the more you efface yourself, are silent, respectful to your neighbor, not insisting on influencing her, the more will you accomplish in souls; on the contrary, the more you assert yourself, enforcing your tastes, your wishes, your methods, your ideas, seeking to convince others . . . the less will you accomplish in souls." *(M.T., no. 310).*

"The mother of a family thinks of her husband and of the care she must give to her children. Each one of you can have many children. Innumerable are the souls in the world who are waiting for the maternal help of your prayers." *(M.T., no. 646).*

"You must have compassion for souls who are nearing their eternity. They must be helped not to have a single bitter feeling, no suspicion of rancor, so that the love of creatures, human love, may open their heart to divine love and to its demands for sincerity." *(M.T., no. 614).*

"A little act of generosity, of patience, of poverty . . . may become treasure that will win a great number of souls to My Heart . . ." *(J.M., p.175).*

"There are some souls that suffer in order to obtain for others strength not to consent to evil. If those two souls had fallen into sin yesterday, they would have been eternally lost. The little acts you did obtained for them the courage to stand firm." Josefa was surprised that such little things could have such vast repercussions. [Jesus answered:] "Yes, My Heart gives divine worth to these little offerings, for what I want is love!" *(J.M., p.196).*

"Do you know what is the masterpiece of creation? It is the creation of souls." *(M.T., no. 381).*

"Give Me love and give Me souls . . ." *(J.M., p.196).*

If you have enjoyed this book, consider making your next selection from among the following . . .

At your Bookdealer or direct from the Publisher.

Prices guaranteed through June 30, 1996.